Living Rich with Coupons

WITH

COUPONS

™

Empowering Smart Shoppers to Live Rich!

Living Rich WITH COUPONS

Empowering Smart Shoppers to Live Rich!

Cindy Livesey

A GENUINE WINDWORD BOOK

ARCHER/RARE BIRD

Archer, 601 West 26th Street, Suite 325, New York, NY 10001
archerlit.com

FIRST TRADE PAPERBACK ORIGINAL EDITION

Printed in the United States
Set in Minion

Publisher's Cataloging-in-Publication data

Livesey, Cindy.

Living rich with coupons : empowering smart shoppers to live rich! / by Cindy Livesey.
pages cm
ISBN 978-1-941729-09-0

1. Coupons (Retail trade). 2. Shopping. 3. Consumer education. I. Title.

TX335 .L56 2015
640.73—dc23

To my husband, Pat, for always being ready and willing to run out to the store at any hour to test a deal. You're the man, and I love you always!

To my kids, you are my world. I would drop anything and everything for you guys...even a promotion for free toilet paper.

To my parents for always being my biggest cheerleaders. Although I think you're really cheering me on so that I continue to build my stockpile and there'll be more stuff for you to "shop" for.

To all the LivingRichWithCoupons.com readers for coming back time and time again!

Contents

Introduction

A M I A MILLIONAIRE? Nope. Far from it. But I feel richer today than I've ever felt in my adult life, and it all started with coupons.

You may be wondering how little pieces of paper with bar codes on them can make a family rich. After all, most people throw them straight in the trash. I used to do that, too. I'd clip a few coupons here and there, put them in my wallet and usually forget to use them, and the other coupons went into the trash. That was back when our family of five lived what we *thought* was a rich life. My husband, Pat, and I had a combined income that topped six figures and we drove new cars, lived in a nice house in an upscale town, and sent our kids to private school. We ate out regularly and overall never really worried about money. Sounds like the perfect life, right? Well, that depends on your definition of *perfect*. Behind our swank lifestyle was a growing mountain of debt. You see, even though we were making good money, we were living well above our means. If we wanted it, we bought it. We didn't search for a frugal way to buy it. We didn't check to see if it was in our budget before we bought it, because we didn't have a budget. I know—crazy, right?! We had all these expensive possessions but they weren't really *ours*. The credit card companies and the banks that lent us money owned most of what we had.

For the average American family, having debt is common and acceptable, even when you're making good money, so I thought we were doing fine right up until I knew we weren't. Pat was the main breadwinner in our family and I had a job but no benefits. In 2007 he lost his job when his company restructured. We were upset, but we were confident that he would find another job. And three months later he did. The new job even offered a slightly higher salary than his previous one. *Phew*, we were glad that didn't last long! We were anxious to get back into our normal spending habits and didn't have a care in the world about our growing debt.

Then it happened. The economy took a nosedive. Businesses were feeling the effects and started tightening their belts by laying off employees. Last one in, first one out. Yup, less than a year after starting his new job, Pat was back in the job market.

Did we think "no big deal" this time? No—we were scared. It was the slap in the face we'd needed, and a hard one at that. Reality began to set in. Our kids were in college, so we had college loan debt, car loans, a mortgage, a second mortgage, and credit card debt along with our regular monthly expenses like utilities, insurance, gas, and groceries. The only equity we had was in our house, and that was dropping quickly. Panic became our motivator, and a huge motivator it was.

The first thing we did was sit down and make a budget. Over the years, we'd talked about making one, but we'd never done it. Bills came in each month and we tried to pay them. If we couldn't, well, some of you may know the drill: take money from one to pay the other. Grocery money was used to pay car loans. We had to eat, so we justified charging our groceries that way.

Wow, just think about that. You buy groceries using a credit card, eat what you bought, and are still paying for it months or maybe even years later. Crazy!

We knew we had to make some drastic changes, so we got out our bank statements and credit card statements for the previous year and reviewed them item by item to see where our money was going. I was shocked when I found that we were spending more than $15,000 a year on groceries alone. *Holy smokes*—$15,000 for a family of five. That was on top of the money we were spending to eat out. Yikes! Boy, did we need to cut that number down. Enter coupons!

For years, I'd been a casual "clipper." You might relate. I clipped coupons when I spotted something I wanted to buy. When I remembered to use them, I'd save a few dollars, which hardly seemed worth the trouble of looking through the coupons in the first place. But now, to get back on our feet, we had to slash our expenses, starting with our huge grocery bill, and that epiphany transformed me from a clipper into a true couponer. I learned the secrets to saving with coupons. I mean *really* saving, not just a dollar here and there. I learned it's not just about clipping and remembering to use those coupons—it's about how and where and when I used them.

It was an awesome feeling to be able to feed my family even though times were tough. I felt empowered! In control!

I began to spread that sense of empowerment across every aspect of our life. We made a strict budget and cut out lots of things, including car loans. We sold our cars and bought less expensive ones, negotiated for the most cost-effective insurance coverage, separated our wants from our needs, and pretty much cut off all unnecessary spending. No eating out, no new clothes, nothing extra.

I'm not going to lie. It was hard, very hard. But at the same time, it felt good. By drastically reducing our spending, we were finding out what was really most important to us. And it wasn't our *stuff.*

After about six months, Pat found another job. It was a happy time for us. We were proud and relieved to have made it through that tough, *not*-so-happy time. But now, with a new source of income, would we go back to our old ways? Not this time! We were determined to stick with our new frugal way of living so we could pay off our debts and start saving. We were committed to being prepared for any unexpected circumstances that might come our way. And after four long years, we did it—we were debt-free. Talk about empowering!

No, it wasn't easy, not in the least, but it was the best thing we've ever done. Learning to live comfortably within our means has turned into living rich frugally!

As I was writing this book, Pat's job vanished in another restructuring, but this time we weren't worried. We knew he could take his time to figure out exactly what he wanted to do. Start a business? Be a consultant? Look for a job? The freedom was his! How great is that?

Today, we wish we'd known from day one of our married life that living a frugal life, below our means, regardless of our financial bracket, would ultimately provide us with the richest life. If we had been couponing and budgeting all along, temporary bouts of unemployment wouldn't have shaken our family as much as they did. But thankfully, those hard lessons brought us to this wonderful financial freedom!

My hope is that you will be empowered like Pat and I were and still are. If you have a job right now, don't put off couponing and budgeting until you lose it. Make changes and take control of your finances now. Whether you have a job and are still struggling to make ends meet or you're unemployed, this book will show you how to turn things around by learning a new way to live. When you set up a budget and learn how to coupon, everything else will fall into place.

Be empowered! Take control! The rewards from the changes you can make are amazing, and very soon you'll be living rich with coupons!

Part One

Couponing for Beginners

Chapter One

What Type of Couponer Are You?

WHETHER YOU'RE BRAND-NEW TO couponing, an experienced couponer saving tons of money at the grocery store, or somewhere in between, you're about to learn how to take your savings to the next level. Throughout my life, I have been at every single level of couponing. I've spent way more than I should have on groceries, throwing away thousands of dollars a year that could have been in my pocket. I've been a clipper, saving a dollar here and there. And I've had short-lived stints where I took couponing seriously but my savings never seemed to be worth the time or effort. My favorite level of couponing is the one I'm at right now. The one that saves me so much money that I was able to pay off all my debt. The one that takes me only about three hours a week to do. Pretty awesome, right?

I started seriously couponing to put food on the table when my husband, Pat, lost his job, and once I got into it, it was easier than I'd thought. So I decided to keep up the couponing after he got another job and use the savings to pay off our debt. And that's exactly what we did. We paid off every dollar we owed! In the process, couponing became my superpower. Wonder Woman has nothing on me!

You may not have that superpower yet, but trust me, you can get it. When my dad was working on our house, he used to say, "If you have the right tools, you can do almost anything." Well, it's the same for couponing. You can use the tools you get from this book to build your superpowers. I mean, even Wonder Woman needs her indestructible bracelets, and you are about to receive yours.

If you're not saving as much as you'd like, you may be wondering, "What am I doing wrong?" Well, there are several levels of couponing. If you're doing any type of couponing at all and saving some money at the grocery store, you're already doing something right. But chances are, you can do even more and save a lot more. The following quiz will help you to see exactly what level of couponing you're on.

What Kind of Couponer Are You?

To find your current couponing level, answer the following questions.

1. I use coupons…

    A. Every now and then
    B. Every week for some of the items on my grocery list
    C. For almost everything I buy at the grocery store
    D. Never

2. My stockpile consists of…

    A. A few items we use often
    B. Is small but growing
    C. Enough toothpaste, shampoo, and deodorant to last a year
    D. What's a stockpile?

3. I get my coupons from…

    A. The Sunday paper when I remember
    B. The Sunday paper every week
    C. Multiple copies of the Sunday paper and lots of printable coupons
    D. What coupons?

4. When I shop, I…

    A. Shop without a list and use some coupons
    B. Shop with a list and also buy other things I see and want
    C. Go with a list and coupons and stick to the list
    D. Shop without a list and buy what I see and want

5. When I need a product for a recipe I'm making, I…

    A. Run to the store and buy the cheapest product I can find (probably the generic brand)
    B. Check my coupons and sales for the week to see if I can find a deal on it
    C. Get it out of my stockpile because it's most likely already there
    D. Run to a convenience store and pay double the price

6. How much do you save each week on your grocery bill?

    A. 10-25%
    B. 25-50%
    C. Over 50%
    D. No clue!

So, how did you do? Let's find out where you stand.

If you answered mostly A's, you're a
COUPON ROOKIE.

You coupon here and there, saving 10 to 25 percent at the grocery store. You spend a few minutes each week scanning the weekly ads and clipping coupons.

If you answered mostly B's, you are a SUPER SAVER.

You save 25 to 50 percent at the grocery store. You like to shop the generic brands in addition to using coupons. You spend about an hour each week scanning the weekly ads and clipping coupons. Your family loves how much you save but secretly wishes you wouldn't come home with all those generic brands.

If you answered mostly C's, you're a
COUPON QUEEN/KING.

You're a serious couponer who saves over 50 percent at the grocery store. You're the queen or king of your stockpile. Your family loves that you save so much but sometimes wonders why you need so much toothpaste. You often donate your excess to those in need, which gives you and your family such pride. You spend about three hours each week scanning the ads, clipping your coupons, and preparing your list. You realize that you couldn't make as much as you save if you worked a part-time job.

If you answered mostly D's, you need a COUPON INTERVENTION.

You aren't saving anything on your grocery bill. As a matter of fact, you probably aren't even looking for deals and are therefore spending way more than you should be. Shopping smart, knowing the sales cycles, and stocking up at the lowest prices are all you need to do to get started. Throw in some coupons and you're on your way to some great savings! Give it a try—I promise you won't be disappointed.

• • •

So now you know where you stand. You know what kind of couponer you are and the kind of couponer you can work toward being. Do you want to get better? Do you want to save even more? Do you want to be able to afford to be a stay-at-home mom or dad? Couponing can do just that. It truly can change your life. So sit back, grab yourself a cup of coffee, and join me in this wonderful world of couponing where you can have the same special couponing superpowers that helped me get my family through unemployment and helped me pay off my debt.

Chapter Two

Couponing Can Change Your Life!

WE ALL HAVE MOMENTS when we suddenly know our lives have been changed forever. Never in my wildest dreams did I think I'd have a life-changing epiphany because of couponing, but I did. Using those little slips of paper strategically delivered us from tons of debt and allowed us to make ends meet during unemployment. And then they helped us to become completely debt-free. If you haven't ever been debt-free, let me tell you something: it's completely life-changing. The fear of not being able to pay the bills? Gone. Yep, gone—because there are no bills. The fear of becoming unemployed again? Gone.

Now, couponing isn't going to do that overnight. It takes time and it takes work, but nothing good in life comes without a little work, right? But this work is fun, rewarding, and exciting. I mean, who wouldn't love to save over 75 percent on their grocery bill in one shopping trip? I'm telling you, once you start saving that kind of money, there's no turning back. Couponing is addictive!

Another big perk of couponing is that you wind up with lots of great name brands in your pantry. Years ago when I was a "clipper" and not a "couponer," I had a lot of store-brand items in my pantry. Don't get me wrong, some store brands are great. There happen to be a few that I love. But some of the best deals are on name brands, which means you can enjoy some of these great brands for much less than store brands cost.

The Magic of Couponing

So MANY OF US can use a little help these days. With salary cuts and higher living costs, sometimes we need that extra part-time job to make ends meet. My solution is to hire yourself as a couponer. The goal of getting a part-time job is to bring additional money into the home. Instead of bringing it in, why not prevent it from going out? That can easily be done with couponing!

How can couponing bring enough money in? Well, let's look at my savings over a year. We were able to save $11,000 in one year on our groceries and it took only about three hours of work a week. My new "part-time job" was paying off to the tune of about $70 an hour. I don't know about you, but if someone asked me if I wanted a job working just three hours a week out of my home whenever I wanted to and could make $70 an hour doing it, I'd jump at the chance.

This way of thinking can be a lifesaver for young parents who are forced to leave their new baby with a sitter so they don't lose that second income. If you're in that boat, consider a new part-time job as a couponer. I know it sounds silly at first to think that couponing can allow you to quit your job to stay home with your children, but look at the money you'll save between the sitter and groceries.

TESTIMONIALS FROM PARENTS

> "I started true couponing in March of 2014, three and a half months before we had our second child. It has truly changed my life and the way I think about spending money and making household purchases. While I always used coupons, couponing is so much different. Couponing has allowed us to stretch our budget and freed me of having to worry about running out to get an item we ran out of. Now I have a stock of all our household essentials for [the same price] I would have paid for one or two items before I became a couponer."
>
> —Robyn Carioti

"I made the choice to transition from a full-time position to a part-time position so that I could be there for my eleven-year-old daughter after school. It meant a big pay cut for my family, but the sacrifice was worth it to spend more time with my family. Because of you and your team and the amazing couponing skills I have acquired, I am able to substantially supplement our finances. Couponing is another source of income."

—Lauren Vivenzio-Borawski

"I've always been a stay-at-home mom, but in 2008, eighteen months after we had our fourth child, my husband lost his job. He worked odd jobs for a few months, and we were really struggling. There were days we had to call his mom to buy us toilet paper. Then one day my sister-in-law called me and said she saw a couponing story on the news and she thought we should try it. I laughed and said, 'Well, you try it, and if it works let me know.' She called back a few weeks later and said, 'It works!'

"So in May 2009, I started couponing and I never looked back. My husband was eventually offered his job back, and we've since had baby number five. We are able to be okay and live only on his income."

—Monica Leal

"Five years ago when my first daughter was one, my husband and I made the decision for me to stop working full-time and work part-time instead. I'm an occupational therapist, and going part-time was going to be a significant change in income for us. But I could no longer bear the thought of a child-care provider seeing my daughter more than I did. So the sacrifice was going to be worth it. Your website was the first that I stumbled upon in my quest to save money. I have two little girls now, and I'm still working part-time. While we don't take the grand vacations we used to take, we have very little debt. When we needed a new furnace, we were able to pay for it in cash. So, thank you, Cindy, for introducing me to this amazing world of savings. What a difference it has made for us. I was able to go part-time stress-free."

—Sandy Gutierrez

"On January 19, 2014, I found out that I'd been blessed with my wish to become a mother. Before my son came along, my husband and I had a budget, but we had a lot of flexibility because we were both working and we had a pretty good combined salary. Two weeks before I delivered, my employer and I finalized a maternity-leave agreement. I worked full-time (forty-plus hours a week) until the moment I went into labor with my son.

"On September 14, 2014, I gave birth to a handsome and healthy baby boy! As soon as I laid my eyes on him I fell in love, and it truly is a feeling you don't know until it happens to you. What a true miracle!

"I took off six weeks and had planned to return to work part-time for one month and then return to work full-time. Two weeks before my return from maternity leave, my employer notified me by mail that my hours had been severely cut. (Because the company had less than fifty employees, it did not have to abide by the Family and Medical Leave Act.)

"With the cost of day care, gas, rent, and bills, I was pretty much forced into quitting my job. I'd been the main breadwinner, and I couldn't figure out how we were going to pay all our bills and put food on the table. I sent out my resume to every place that was hiring within the tri-state area. I couldn't enjoy my tiny miracle because I was so worried about how I was going to afford to take care of him. I felt hopeless.

"Two weeks later, I stumbled upon your Facebook page, which led me to your website. I was amazed at all the money you saved and was completely knocked off my feet that you were able to find ways to get items completely free! The most helpful posts were/are the diapers! You never really believe how much you go through until you're actually a parent and go through it! Just the other day I went to Babies 'R' Us and got my forty-pack of diapers for just $2.98. You'd better believe I stocked up that day!

"Because of coupons and the help of your website, not only did I not have to go back to work, but our savings account is at an all-time high. It may sound silly, but I thank God every day for stumbling upon your Facebook page and the complete miracle coupons have worked for my family and me. Spending every day with my son and being able to watch him grow has been the best thing that has ever happened to me. So, thank you so much for your couponing advice and sharing the deals that you find! Thank you for the time with my son!"

—Sophia Ettinger

Entering this crazy world of couponing can literally change your life and your lifestyle! You'll start making ends meet, pay off your debt, create a financial cushion, and feel freer and happier than you've felt in years, maybe decades. That is living rich with coupons!

Not only does couponing save you money, but it also helps you to manage your money and be more disciplined with it. Since we started couponing, we have really questioned every purchase, large and small, that we make. Many times the answer is "You know what? We really don't need that." Before I buy something, I ask myself, "What if I didn't have that object in my life? Would I be happy without it? Would having it change my life in some way?" If the answer is no, I usually pass on it. And you know what? I really didn't need it. We can learn to live with so much less and actually be happier that way.

People Who Swear by Couponing!

TWENTY-FIVE YEARS AGO, DOMINIC immigrated to America from Naples, Italy, with just a duffel bag and a heart full of dreams. He put himself through school and obtained his master's degree in teaching. After working as a foreign-language teacher for fourteen years, budget cuts in his school district forced the layoff of twenty-one teachers, including Dominic.

He and his wife, Jamie, had just purchased a house, and with no hope of getting his job back, he started teaching Italian at the local college. He received very little unemployment compensation since he chose to work, but the job wasn't paying enough to make ends meet. "The bills were piling up and I had no way to pay them," he said. His wife had a secretarial job that didn't pay very well, but at least it provided them both with health insurance.

He was upset and depressed and had many sleepless nights. He worried about the future of his family and his son, Nicola, who was two years old at the time. He and Jamie had been married for only a few years when he lost his job. "I felt like someone had pulled the rug from under me," he said. "There were days that we could not put food on the table. I even asked for help from my family overseas with much embarrassment." He was working four part-time jobs and it still wasn't enough.

One day, Dominic saw the show *Extreme Couponing*, and that led him to go online and look for information about couponing. That's when he discovered LivingRichWithCoupons.com. "It was the day after my birthday that I found your website," he said, "and since then I have consulted it every day for tips, purchases, and advice. There is no better site than yours out there, and I am telling you this with sincerity. I will never forget my first trip as a couponer. Jamie and I went to Walgreens, bought a package of Stayfree pads for two dollars and received two dollars in rewards. We used the rewards to buy milk and we got all excited. I went back to buy more pads at least six times that week. We ended up with enough to last at least six months. I will never forget that experience."

Since then, Dominic and Jamie have become the king and queen of coupons for their friends and family. They have created quite a stockpile, and couponing has allowed them to share with friends and family and donate to disabled children and their families. After struggling for four years, Dominic got a full-time job as a foreign-language teacher in another district. But he didn't stop couponing.

> "Couponing is a way of life now," he said. "My wife and I are a team. I do the research and the printing, and together with our son we cut the coupons. Jamie goes to the local drugstores, and once a week we drive an hour to Shoprite, our favorite store, to get groceries. This weekend we saved $140 and just paid $2.
>
> "When I bring home fifteen to twenty bags of groceries a week, my eyes and my heart are filled with joy. I quickly call my mom in Italy to

tell her how much I saved and what I bought. I even taught my son that we don't purchase things without coupons."

Dominic and his family are living rich with coupons! And they're not the only ones. Here are a few letters from other couponing converts:

"In 2011, my son was born and I had to take a hiatus from clipping coupons. I wasn't couponing in an extreme way, but my mother-in-law would save her coupon inserts for me and I would collect the ones I knew I'd use. I ended up having a very high-maintenance baby, lots of stress, and a husband who worked about twenty hours a day five or six days a week. Needless to say, we were *not* saving money.

"At the end of 2011, my husband lost his job, and I started to coupon more effectively but also started using credit cards to supplement our much lower income, not even thinking of the future. He was out of work for a year, and we depleted our savings, so with our newfound credit card debt, it was more important than ever to start focusing on coupons.

"I found this site sometime during 2012. I sang praises to the gods! I was able to cut our grocery bill from $100 a week, to about $50 a week. Of course, there are weeks when I spend more but many weeks that I can easily spend less because I won't need to shop—I shop the stockpile those weeks.

"Essentially, I stopped using credit cards to pay for groceries. I often have Catalinas and rain checks to cover a good portion of my groceries now. I spend about $30 every three to four months on ink, and I save more than that in one shopping trip per week.

"This has really helped us keep our credit card debt under control, and now I am conditioned to stick to my shopping lists and only get what may be on sale whenever possible. With a kid in diapers, *still* spending fifty dollars a week (including his diapers and wipes) is something that makes me so happy. It's almost become a hobby, and I am able to share my stockpile with my college-age sister-in-law and my unemployed mother. Even if I save her only ten dollars a week for things she needs, it makes me feel good."

—Deena

"I live in New Jersey, I am a proud homemaker, and by using coupons I was able to feel like I had a part-time job at home. I would save hundreds of dollars every month and would donate food to our local church food bank. After about two years of using coupons, I saved enough money that when my husband became sick and had to stop working, and then found out he had cancer, I was able to keep my family in 'the black.' We had to wait six months to get approved for social security disability. In the meantime I had been able save enough money in case of emergency to keep us afloat for two years. I am still able to stay home and take care of my family and make ends meet using your website. I tell everyone at the grocery store about you, and my mom is now hooked. We don't know how we ever shopped without you, *Lol!* I not only use your site for groceries but for any shopping... I have learned so much about being an informed and smart consumer. I have always been good with money and was the type of girl that only bought things on sale, but LRWC [Living Rich With Coupons] takes this to the next level, *lol*! I have *no debt* and I owe it all to you!

"My family truly appreciates the knowledge I have gained from LRWC."

—Melanie P.

"Thanks to you and your team, I have financial peace of mind I have never had before."

—Brenda

"I have always loved coupons, but up until February it was always just, 'Oh, great, I have a coupon for that' and I would save a little. I watched the *Extreme Couponing* show and would always say, 'I wish it was possible in New York.' But with the price of groceries here and the lack of discount supermarkets, it seemed like it could never happen. Then I discovered LivingRichWithCoupons.com and suddenly realized that you can get things for free and ridiculously cheap even here. It was also at that same time that I found a Facebook group that helps families in need. I have been using my couponing skills to get things to help feed families who otherwise would have very little food. I started with a goal of ten to fifteen dollars a month and have been able to purchase as many as 156 items with that amount of money. I have gotten so good at it that the director of the group is now giving me money to do the shopping for the group."

—Rebecca

"Because of the money we have saved, one, we can pay bills we wouldn't have been able to pay otherwise, and two, my children can participate in sports, viola lessons, and Boy Scouts, most of which they probably wouldn't have been able to do without the couponing!!

"I've been out of work since January, and needless to say, money is tight. I've saved over $3,000 this year with your help, and it has meant my children can eat nutritiously while developing great life habits."

—Mary

Chapter Three

Couponing Myths

THERE ARE A LOT of myths and misconceptions about couponing, and if you believe them, they can stop you from saving money. I'm here to help you sort out the confusion so you know what coupons can really do and just how easy it can be to save a small fortune by using them.

#1 Myth: I can't buy healthy food with coupons

I HEAR THIS MYTH over and over again and it's simply not true. Yes, there are a lot of coupons for processed foods, but there are also coupons for meat and poultry, produce, dairy products, and healthy snacks. Sign up for healthy brands' newsletters and "like" their Facebook pages. Better yet, contact the company directly to let them know you're interested in trying their products. Some companies will send you coupons to give their products a try.

Even the mainstream coupon sites such as Coupons.com and RedPlum.com are offering more and more coupons for dairy products, meat, nuts, fruits, and vegetables. But be sure to visit sites like MamboSprouts.com or CommonKindness.com for even more healthy food coupons.

#2 Myth: You need to turn your house into a mini-market

STOCKING UP IS NOT at all like hoarding. You don't need to stock up as if a natural disaster is looming. You don't need your living room to look like a mini-mart. Stocking up with about three months' worth of your family's favorite items is all you need to do. Since sales and coupons cycle around about every eight to twelve weeks, there will be plenty of opportunities to take advantage of sales over and over again. There's no need to give up your living room!

#3 Myth: Couponing is a full-time job

THE AMOUNT OF TIME you put into couponing is totally up to you. Contrary to popular belief, it doesn't take much time to save a lot. I spend about two hours each week preparing for my shopping trip and clipping coupons. And the shopping trip itself takes less time with a prepared list.

Before couponing, I usually went to the grocery store without a plan. Other times I had a plan in mind but didn't stick to it. It took me at least an hour in the store, shopping every aisle, checking to see what I needed or wanted. Sound familiar?

Once you get a few months of couponing under your belt and have started to build a nice stockpile of your family's favorite and most-used items, your shopping trips will be much shorter. The goal is to go prepared, with list and coupons in hand, and stick to your plan. You spend a bit more time preparing for your shopping trip but a lot less time in the store.

Here's a breakdown of my time before and after coupons:

My Shopping Time Before Couponing

- Preparing for shopping trip, looking through the sales circular, and writing up a quick list: 15 minutes
- Shopping: 1.5 hours
- Second trip to the store because I forgot to buy something I need: 30 minutes
- Third trip to the store because I forgot to buy something else I need: 30 minutes

Total time spent preparing and shopping: 2 hours 45 minutes

My Shopping Time After Coupons:

- Preparing for my shopping trip, looking through the circular, clipping coupons, and making a detailed list: 2 hours
- Shopping at one store: 30 minutes
- Shopping at a second store: 30 minutes

Total time spent preparing and shopping: 3 hours

What's the time difference there? Fifteen minutes—that's it. It takes me about fifteen minutes more to use coupons and save thousands.

Yes, it will take longer in the beginning, but don't let that discourage you. It will take less time and come easier to you the more you do it. Plus, throughout the book, I explain exactly how to do it so you can create a system that works well for you.

#4 Myth: Store brands are always cheaper than name brands

THIS IS ONE OF my favorite myths to dispel. I once read an article on a very popular finance site called "7 Things You Should Always Buy Generic." I made a side-by-side comparison as to why buying brand names with coupons was often more affordable than buying generic.

Sample Cost Comparison[1]

1. Pain relievers and other over-the-counter
    medications

Their list:

Name-Brand Acetaminophen: $10.99

Store-Brand Acetaminophen: $6.99

Save $4 (36 percent) by buying store brand

My List:

Store-Brand Acetaminophen: $6.99

Excedrin: $0.99 after coupon & ECB (ExtraCare
 Bucks) at CVS

Save $6 (86 percent) by buying name brand

2. Water

Their List:

Name-Brand Water: $1.25

Store-Brand Water: $0.85

Save $0.40 (32 percent) by buying store brand

---

[1]   Prices and deals were valid at the time of my comparison.

My List:

Store-Brand Water: $0.85

Poland Spring: $0.50 for an eight-pack or four six-packs after coupon & Catalina offer

Save as much as $0.85 (100 percent) by buying name brand

3. Milk

Their List:

Name-Brand Milk: $5.45

Store-Brand Milk: $3.39

Save $2.06 (38 percent) by buying store brand

My list:

Store-Brand Milk: $3.39

Smart Balance Milk: 4 quarts free + $1 Moneymaker after coupon & Catalina offer

Save $4.49 (129 percent) by buying name brand

4. Margarine

Their List:

Name-Brand Margarine: $1.79

Store-Brand Margarine: $1.19

Save $0.60 (34 percent) by buying store brand

My List:

Store-Brand Margarine: $1.19

Land O'Lakes Buttery Spread: free after coupon

Save $1.19 (100 percent) by buying name brand

5.   Bleach

Their List:

Name-Brand Bleach: $2.25

Store-Brand Bleach: $1.67

Save $0.58 (26 percent) by buying store brand

My List:

Store-Brand Bleach: $1.67

Clorox Bleach: $0.65 each after Catalina

Save $1.02 (61 percent) by buying name brand

6.   Cleaning Products

Their List:

Name-Brand Cleaner With Bleach: $3.29

Store-Brand Cleaner With Bleach: $2.39

Save $0.90 (27 percent) by buying store brand

<u>My List:</u>
Store-Brand Cleaner With Bleach: $2.39
Lysol Products: free after coupon & Catalina
Save $2.39 (100 percent) by buying name brand

7. Spices

<u>Their List:</u>
Name-Brand Oregano: $5.48 per ounce
Store-Brand Oregano: $1.24 per ounce
Save $4.24 (77 percent) by buying store brand

<u>My List:</u>
Store-Brand Oregano: $1.24 per ounce
McCormick Oregano: $0.85 per ounce after coupon
Save $0.39 (31 percent) and pay almost nothing for
   name brand

Myth #5: The savings aren't worth the effort

IF YOU'RE JUST USING a few coupons here and there without a couponing strategy, then you're right, it's probably not worth the effort. But with the strategies you'll learn in this book, the savings are more than worth the effort. The first thing you're going to do with each coupon is wait for the product to go on sale. Let's say you have a coupon for

$0.25 off a $4 can of nuts. Instead of using the coupon, you hold on to it until the nuts are on sale for $2. Then you can buy them for $1.75 and save $2.25. And if there are stores that double coupons in your area, you can get $0.50 off with that coupon, making the nuts just $1.50!

But wait, stack a sale with a store coupon or promotion for, say, another $1 in savings. Now, after the sale, the doubled coupon, and the $1 store promotion or store coupon, you've gotten the nuts for just $0.50! You saved $3.50! Hello! Now that's what I'm talkin' about!

If you're thinking, "Yeah, right, like that would ever happen," think again because it happens all the time. LivingRichWithCoupons.com will alert you about all those types of deals.

So don't bother using a $0.25 coupon on a $4 product. It's not worth it. But stack up those extra savings and you've got yourself a winner of a deal.

Myth #6: Couponing just doesn't work

IF COUPONING ISN'T SAVING you the kind of money you think you should be saving, my guess is you haven't been doing it long enough. The first three to four weeks of couponing is when you're figuring everything out. Finding the best sales, finding the stores with the best prices, and building up your stock of coupons. You're also building up your stockpile during those first weeks.

If you don't have a stock of items your family uses often, the prices you pay at the grocery store are being dictated by the grocery store. So your price points are much higher. Once you stock up, the amount you're willing to pay will go down because you can be patient and wait for a better sale, a better coupon, or both!

During the first month of couponing, you won't notice much of a decrease in the amount you're spending, but you will see that you're bringing in more products than you used to. Around the four-week mark, you'll start to notice you're spending less on your groceries. By the time you hit twelve weeks of steady couponing, your savings will be amazing. There will even be weeks you don't have to shop.

Nothing good happens overnight. Successful couponing takes time, work, and planning. So be patient and work at it and you'll reap the great rewards that will financially benefit you and your family.

Myth #7: Saving money with coupons takes extreme measures

IF YOU'VE WATCHED THE show *Extreme Couponing*, get everything you've seen on that show out of your mind. Nobody needs to buy a hundred containers of Tic Tacs or a pallet of toothpaste. Not only do you not need to buy that much, but stores don't allow that type of couponing, since there are usually restrictions on the amount of coupons you can use when shopping. The shoppers on that show have gathered coupons from tons of sources. They've even bought them and dumpster-dived for them!

Don't let shows like that make you think that's the way you have to shop and save. It's not. What you need to do is take your time and stock up on the things that are important to your family. If you do that, you will amaze yourself with how much you can save.

Chapter Four

Getting Started

"The expert in anything was once a beginner."
—Helen Hayes, the first lady of American theater

A RE YOU READY TO save? Are you ready to start keeping that hard-earned money in your pocket? I know I sure was. Whether you have no choice but to save because of unemployment or a cut in pay or you're just tired of spending so much money on your groceries, this is as good a time as any to cut that grocery bill in half.

But I know what you're asking, because I asked the same question myself: Where in the world do I begin? It seems overwhelming, I know, and it *is* a little confusing at first. But I'm here for you. I want you to be where I am right now—saving thousands of dollars a year—so we're in this together. And remember, an expert was once a beginner; I was once a beginner just like you.

When I started couponing, I approached it like a new job. Think back to your first day on a new job. You were introduced to everyone, told about the company policies, shown your new desk or work space, and trained for your new position. At the end of the first day, your head was spinning. All those names to remember, and you had so many questions: When am I allowed to take a lunch break? What did they say I was supposed to do with those files? Are the task reports due every Friday or every Monday? But by the end of the week, you were starting to find your way around the office, remembered a few names, and could even do some of your new job responsibilities on your own. Within a month, you were feeling really comfortable, continuing to learn new things but on your way to being a valued team member for the company.

Those are the same stages you'll go through with couponing. In the beginning, you'll need to learn the coupon lingo much like you'd have to learn your coworkers' names. You'll have to understand coupon policies. You'll have to set up a place to work to keep yourself organized. You'll start with small steps and build your skills just like you did with your tasks at a new company. But the great thing about this "job" is that it's rewarding and fun. And you can do it whenever you want—when the kids are sleeping, on the weekends, or while you're waiting to pick up your kids at soccer or dance. You run your "company." You choose your hours.

So let's jump in and get going. First, let me tell you that you have this fantastic, time-saving tool that wasn't around when I started couponing. It's a website that does all the work for you. Well, it doesn't actually do the shopping for you, but LivingRichWithCoupons.com tells you exactly what the sales are at many different stores and matches up the available coupons you can use to save the most money. And get this—it's free to use! Pretty awesome, right? My site is a huge time-saver for people who are serious about saving money. So be sure to check out the site to familiarize yourself with the deals and coupons that are posted each day.

Learning the Names

LET'S START WITH LEARNING the lingo. Yes, couponing actually does have its own lingo. For example, we don't call a "Buy One Get One Free" sale or coupon by its full name. We lovingly refer to it as BOGO. We refer to Internet-printed coupons as IPs because, well, it's just easier.

Coupon Lingo Cheat Sheet

Copy this and keep it handy until you remember them all!

Blinkie: Nickname for Red Smart Source machines found in most stores. They are those little red boxes that hang from store shelves and dispense coupons.

B1G1/BOGO: Buy one, get one free.

BOGO 50%: Buy one, get one 50 at percent off.

CAT: Catalina coupons that the cashier prints in the store. Not every store offers these coupons, but most of the larger regional grocery stores do. You've probably received these coupons when checking out. The machines are provided and operated by a company called Catalina Marketing.

DND: Do not double.

ECB: ExtraCare Bucks from CVS.

IP: Internet-printed coupon.

ISO: In search of…

MIR: Mail-in rebate.

Mfg: Manufacturer coupon.

MM: Moneymaker.

NLA: No longer available.

OOP: Out of pocket.

OYNO: On your next order.

P&G: Procter & Gamble insert.

psa: Prices start at.

PP: Price plus from Shoprite.

RP: RedPlum insert.

RR: Register Rewards (Walgreens).

SCR: Single check rebate (Rite Aid).

SS: SmartSource insert.

UPC: Universal Product Code.

Wags: Walgreens.

Tear Pads: Coupon pads located in stores to promote products.

YMMV: Your miles may vary (when talking about your particular store as compared with another store).

WYB: When you buy.

$1/2: $1 off of two items.

Understand Coupon Policies

WHEN YOU STARTED YOUR new job, you may have been given a company policy handbook. In couponing, your company handbook is made up of your stores' coupon policies. Understanding each store's coupon policy is an important first step in using coupons effectively.

Knowing the policies:

1. Ensures that you know how to correctly use coupons at each store.

2. Allows you to take advantage of every possible savings you can at that store.

For instance, did you know you can stack, or pair, a store coupon with a manufacturer coupon at Target? Did you know you can use a coupon on a free product at CVS? Let me give you an example. Let's say CVS has a BOGO sale. You can use a coupon on each item in the sale, even the free one. This is one way that using coupons wisely can actually help you to make money!

By reading and understanding the coupon policies for the stores you shop at the most, you're able to take full advantage of everything those stores have to offer in savings. In the resource section at the end of the book, I list all the major policies that were valid at the time this book was published, but I highly recommend visiting stores' websites to be sure you have the most current policy available.

Set Up Your Work Space

YOUR NEW COUPONING SPACE doesn't have to be anything grand or fancy. A file box, scissors, and a notebook with your coupon policies are all you need. Your work space can be at your kitchen or dining room table or on a coffee table. You just need some place where you can clip your coupons, plan your shopping trip, and stay organized.

I have a desk with a computer. I use a file storage box to keep my coupons from the Sunday paper. In the storage box, I also have a folder that I keep my Internet-printed coupons in. That's it! My own little coupon heaven.

Start Small and Build

DURING YOUR FIRST MONTH at your new job, did you rewrite the procedures manual for the company, run your first meeting, or take full control of an assembly line? Probably not. You were introduced to the tasks and built up your responsibilities slowly from there. This is exactly how to approach couponing. Start small. Don't try to do everything at once. You can't be the coupon queen or king overnight. It's just not going to happen. You'll burn out and get overwhelmed.

I started out by shopping at one store and one store only, CVS. I decided to master my couponing skills and learn that store's policy inside and out. I was able to feel confident and I became a couponing expert there in a very short time. I quickly built up a nice stockpile (we'll talk about the importance of a stockpile in Chapter Eight) of health and beauty products, household products, and even some food items. I was on my way to great savings from just a few weeks of shopping at one store. At that point, I was ready to put my newfound knowledge and confidence to use at other stores, including my local grocery store.

So choose the store where you'd like to start. It can be a drugstore, your local grocery store, or even a national chain store like Target or Walmart. Master that store. Learn and understand its coupon policies and then move on from there. Start small and build!

Set Goals

LET'S LOOK AT SOME goals you'd like to accomplish by couponing and how much time you'd like to spend on your new "job." If you're like me, you'll continually tweak and change your goals. That's okay as long as you know where you're headed. Writing down goals for yourself can keep you headed in the right direction.

Answer the following questions so you know exactly what you want to gain from couponing.

1. How much time do you want to spend couponing each week? After years of couponing, I spend three hours a week and save over 75 percent on my groceries.

2. How much money do you want to save each week/ month/year? This is the only goal I write down for myself. The first year, I said I needed to save $7,000 a year, and I exceeded my goal by saving nearly $11,000. So set a realistic goal for the year and then break it down by the month so you can track how you're doing.

Where, When, How, and Stock Up

I KNOW YOU'RE EXCITED to save. Your goals are set, you have a small work space for yourself, and you can taste the savings. I'm excited for you, too! I remember that feeling, so I know you can't wait to get going. In Part Two, besides showing you how you can buy healthy food without spending a fortune, I cover the four-part couponing strategy. We'll tackle:

- Where to find coupons
- When to use your coupons
- How to use your coupons
- How to stock up

So put your thinking cap on because you are about to learn the true secrets to savings.

Part Two

Turn On Your Couponing Superpowers!

GETTING STARTED WITH COUPONS!

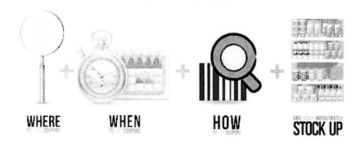

WHERE   WHEN   HOW   STOCK UP

Chapter Five

Where to Get Coupons

Let's talk about where to get those little pieces of paper that are, in my opinion, just like cash. Yep, cash! Just think, you can open your Sunday newspaper and clip cash. Or you can print cash from the Internet. And guess what—the feds aren't going to lock you up for it. It's the only time you can print money from your computer legally! That's the way I look at it anyway.

So, where do we get coupons? There are a ton of sources. Here are some of them:

Inserts in Your Weekly Paper

Every Saturday or Sunday, newspapers are filled with hundreds of dollars' worth of coupons. The inserts are put out by Smart Source, RedPlum, or Proctor & Gamble.

Some weeks a newspaper will have one insert and other weeks there can be as many as five inserts! There are also a few weekends each year when newspapers don't have any coupon inserts. This usually occurs during holiday weekends.

Printable Coupons

THE INTERNET IS A wonderful source for coupons that can be printed right from your computer. There are many sources, including:

- Coupons.com
- SmartSource.com
- RedPlum.com
- Hopster.com
- CommonKindness.com
- MamboSprouts.com

Another great source for Internet coupons is the brands themselves. If you have a Facebook page, you can like different brands so you can be alerted of any new coupons they have available. The great thing about these Facebook coupons is that they're usually higher-value coupons. The bad thing is that these coupons are usually limited and can be printed only two times per computer. To start printing these coupons, you usually have to download the site's coupon-printing software. This software is required because codes are printed on each coupon for security. Remember how I told you it's like printing cash? Well, here's a great example. The brands embed codes in the coupons so they can be sure coupons aren't copied. Copying coupons that have been printed from the Internet is illegal.

Catalina Coupons

THESE COUPONS ARE USUALLY printed as manufacturer coupons and also have the store's logo on them. They are meant to be used at the store where you receive them, but sometimes you can use these coupons at other stores. For instance, I shop at Shoprite stores. They allow us to use Catalina manufacturer coupons that were printed at a different store even though the coupons have the other store's logo on them. This is another reason to learn the coupon policies of the stores where you shop. If there are stores in your area that accept Catalinas from other stores, it's another great opportunity to save.

Coupons in Magazines

MANY OF THE POPULAR women's magazines such as *Better Homes & Gardens*, *Shape*, and *Woman's Day* have coupons each month. One magazine that's very popular with couponers is *All You*. Of all the magazines, that's the one that offers the most coupons.

Tear Pads/Blinkies

HAVE YOU EVER SPOTTED a coupon in a store that made a product free? I have. You may have noticed the little red coupon machines, or blinkies, that hang off the shelf at your local store. You know the ones—you pull a coupon out and wait a few seconds and another one appears. Well, one time I got a blinkie for $1 off any Barilla pasta sauce. And guess what—Barilla pasta sauce was on sale for just $0.99. Bingo—free!

Now, that doesn't always happen, but be sure to keep your eye out for those coupons. There may not be a good deal on that product when you get the coupon, but hold on to it. You never know when a great sale will pop up.

The same goes for tear pad coupons. You can usually find these attached to displays in the store.

eCoupons

DIGITAL COUPONS, ALSO KNOWN as eCoupons, are growing in popularity every year. These coupons are electronically "loaded" onto your store loyalty cards. Some stores will even allow you to use them right from your smartphone. Be sure to check with your local stores to see what types of options are available.

eCoupons are easy and convenient to use. They can usually be used only one time but check your store's policy.

Buying More Than One Newspaper Each Week

NOW THAT YOU KNOW all the places to get coupons, let's talk about how many coupons you should have. Back when I first went from a coupon clipper to a true couponer, I knew I needed to have more than one Sunday paper in order to make the most of my savings. I can still remember my husband's reaction when I asked him to buy four newspapers and he asked me which ones I wanted him to buy.

"Buy four of the *Star Ledger*," I said (this was our local paper at the time).

"Wait, you want four of the same exact paper?" he said.

"Yep. Trust me, I'm going to make this couponing thing work."

As he walked to the car shaking his head, I hoped I was right because it did seem a bit silly to buy four newspapers. It may seem like you're defeating the purpose—which is to save money—but believe me, it will soon pay off!

After about four weeks of buying multiple papers each weekend and printing from the Internet, I started to see my spending at the grocery store drop. At that point, I realized that the "investment" I was making on those newspapers and ink for the printable coupons was just that: an investment in my new job of saving money. My savings far outweighed my expenses, which in my book makes couponing a great investment.

But I know what you are thinking: Why do you need multiple papers? The answer is simple (and will be covered in full detail in Chapter Eight): so you can stock up. If you're able to purchase something for free or 90 percent off using a coupon, would it make sense to buy just one of those items? No way! Stock up! That's why you need more coupons. Trust me—it will all make sense once you read the next few chapters.

Organizing Your Coupons

Keeping your coupons organized will help to keep the time you spend couponing to a minimum. There's nothing worse than opening your weekly circular to see a great sale on a product and know you have a coupon—in a big pile somewhere.

Finding the best way to organize your coupons is important. There's no right or wrong way, but it has to be a way that makes it quick and easy to find the ones you want. Here are a few suggested methods to help get you started:

1. **Coupon binders**

Many new couponers like to use a coupon binder. The binder is simply a three-ring binder, usually with a zipper compartment. Inside are baseball-card inserts that are separated by categories. These categories can be set up like your grocery store aisles or by product categories (i.e., frozen, dairy, cleaning, pet, etc.).

The bad thing about the coupon binder method of organizing is that every Sunday you have to cut all or most of your coupons and place them in your binder. This can be time-consuming, though it's also a fun activity for the kids.

The good thing about the coupon binder is that it has all your coupons in one place and you can take the entire binder with you to the store.

2. **Filing whole inserts**

Filing your inserts whole is an easy and great way to keep those coupons organized. This method is super-easy and simply requires a file drawer or portable file box.

When you get your coupon inserts, you just write the date on the front of the inserts and place them in a hanging folder that's also dated. Three months' worth of coupons is about all you need to keep in the folder.

This is the method I use now, but it's effective only if you plan on using LivingRichWithCoupons.com to plan your shopping trips. That's because, since you aren't clipping coupons, you don't know which coupons you have available. However, if you use the match-ups on LivingRichWithCoupons.com, the date of the insert is listed in the match-ups, making it a snap to find the coupons.

Select All / Clear Selection

• WALMART •

Chi-Chi's Salsa, 16oz - $1.78 (rollback price)
$1/1 Chi-Chi's Salsa Product, 16oz or larger (77477)
as low as $0.78 after coupon

3. **Other filing systems**
- Organize your coupons in a canceled check file.
- Organize your coupons in a recipe card file or old shoe box.
- Use expandable files

Other resources for coupons:

- Libraries sometimes have swap boxes, or you can set one up in an organization that you belong to.

- Friends, coworkers, and members of online groups you can trade coupons with.

- Doctors' and dentists' offices sometimes have coupons in their waiting rooms.

Now that you know where to get your coupons and how to keep them neatly organized, you're ready to find out *when* to use those coupons. This next step is the step that turns on those couponing superpowers and takes you from a coupon clipper to a couponer! Come on—let's see how much we can save together.

Chapter Six

When to Use Coupons

MANY YEARS AGO, WHEN I just clipped a few coupons here and there, I wasn't saving enough money to justify the time I was spending trying to save. Then, when my husband lost his job and we were faced with either spending our money on feeding our family or keeping a roof over our heads, I figured out that magic formula for saving on our groceries. And it didn't just involve clipping. I discovered that the magic came from knowing *when* to use those coupons.

Now, in retrospect, knowing when to use coupons seems like something I should have realized all along. But truth be told, most people don't give it much thought. Once I figured out what I was doing wrong and made that one small change, those couponing superpowers kicked in.

So, when do you use your coupons? There are three important tactics that will determine when you use your coupons:

- Wait for a sale
- Follow sales cycles
- Buy at the lowest price

I know, you're sitting there saying, "Well, hello. That's pretty obvious." I agree. I thought the same thing. However, most people don't follow that formula.

My previous attempt at couponing went something like this: Sunday morning I would open the newspaper and see what coupons were available for that weekend. I'd flip through the inserts and see a coupon for the cereal we used, the string cheese the kids liked, the toilet paper I liked to buy, and our favorite salsa. I'd clip those coupons, put them into an envelope, and take them with me to the store the next time I stopped in.

Sometimes before I went shopping, I would prepare a list, working with the weekly flier that came in the mail. Armed with my list, the flier, and the coupons I'd just clipped, I'd head to the store.

At the store, I made my way down every aisle, browsing and selecting items to put in my cart. I would feel confident that I was getting good prices because I would compare prices from the shelf tag to be sure I selected something that was at the lower price, which meant I had a lot of store brands in my cart. I'd also be sure to pick up the items I had coupons for.

At checkout, my total would be $250 to $300 for the week for a family of five. Yikes!

So, what did I do wrong? I'd gotten so excited about saving a dollar on string cheese that my kids wanted, another dollar on the cereal we love, and fifty cents on toilet paper that I never gave a thought to waiting for those items to be at their lowest prices.

Let me show you a breakdown of how waiting for a great sale before you use your coupons can make a huge dent in your grocery bill.

PRICE:

cereal $3.99 = $3.99

cereal $3.99 − $1.00 = $2.99

cereal $2.50 − $1.00 = $1.50

cereal $2.50 − $1.00 − "1" Store Coupon or Promotion = $.50 STOCK UP!

Take a look at the image on the previous page. The first line is the cereal's full retail price of $3.99. The second line is full retail price using a $1 coupon, making it just $2.99. The next line is the sale price of $2.50 minus that $1 coupon, making it just $1.50. But the last line is the line you need to focus on. It's where the magic happens. Or, as I like to think of it, where your couponing superpowers kick in. That last line takes advantage of not only a sale but also a store coupon and/or a store promotion, making the cereal only $0.50 a box. *Fifty cents a box.* Not $2.99 or even $1.50 a box. That's a huge price difference, and trust me, those savings add up quickly.

Follow Sales Cycles

ALSO, LITTLE DID I know that sales on products usually run in cycles. Those cycles, although not set in stone, run about every eight to twelve weeks. So that box of cereal that went on sale for just $2.50 and was matched up with a store promotion and coupons most likely won't go on sale like that again for another two to three months. That's why we need to stock up at that super-low price.

We also want to keep in mind the sales cycles that involve holidays and events throughout the year. For instance, snack and finger foods always go on sale around the

Super Bowl. Candy goes on sale in February for Valentine's Day. Baking products go on sale during November for the holidays. Barbecue sauce and condiments go on sale in May and June for the summer months.

Here's a list of seasonal produce and what goes on sale when:

January Seasonal Produce:
- Avocados
- Broccoli
- Brussels sprouts
- Cabbage
- Cauliflower
- Celery
- Leeks
- Kiwi
- Grapefruit
- Lemons
- Oranges
- Papayas
- Tangelos
- Tangerines

January Sale Items:

- Diet foods
- Eggs
- Tea
- Snack foods
- Soda

February Seasonal Produce:

- Asparagus
- Artichokes
- Broccoli
- Carrots
- Cauliflower
- Potatoes
- Spinach
- Avocados
- Grapefruit
- Kiwi
- Lemons
- Oranges
- Papaya

February Sale Items:

- Canned products
- Chocolate

- Hot breakfast products (frozen waffles, oatmeal, etc.)
- Low-cholesterol products
- Soy sauce
- Stir-fry mix
- Teriyaki

March Seasonal Produce:
- Asparagus
- Broccoli
- Cabbage
- Carrots
- Celery
- Lettuce
- Potatoes
- Mangoes
- Pineapples

March Sale Items:
- Corned beef
- Frozen foods

April Seasonal Produce:
- Asparagus
- Artichokes
- Broccoli

- Carrots
- Lettuce
- Onions
- Rhubarb
- Spring peas
- Zucchini
- Avocados
- Mangoes
- Pineapple

April Sale Items:
- Baking products
- Eggs
- Food coloring/dyes
- Jewish/Passover foods
- Organic foods

May Seasonal Produce:
- Artichokes
- Asparagus
- Beets
- Broccoli
- Carrots
- Green beans
- Lettuce

- Okra
- Rhubarb
- Spring peas
- Zucchini
- Blackberries
- Raspberries
- Strawberries

May Sale Items:
- Condiments
- Grilling meats
- Hamburger/hot dog buns
- Salad dressing
- Snacks
- Soda

June Seasonal Produce:
- Corn
- Cucumbers
- Eggplant
- Red onions
- Summer squash
- Sweet Vidalia onions
- Tomatoes
- Apricots

- Blackberries
- Blueberries
- Cherries
- Grapes
- Honeydew
- Nectarines
- Peaches
- Raspberries
- Strawberries
- Watermelon

June Sale Items:
- Condiments
- Dairy products
- Popsicles
- Grilling meats
- Hamburger/hot dog buns

July Seasonal Produce:
- Corn
- Cucumbers
- Eggplant
- Garlic
- Green beans
- Okra

- Peppers
- Potatoes
- Red onions
- Summer squash
- Tomatoes
- Blueberries
- Figs
- Grapes
- Nectarines
- Peaches
- Pears
- Plums
- Watermelon

July Sale Items:
- Baked beans
- Condiments
- Grilling meats
- Hamburger/hot dog buns

August Seasonal Produce:
- Beans
- Corn
- Cucumbers
- Eggplant

- Okra
- Onions
- Peppers
- Tomatoes
- Avocados
- Berries
- Figs
- Grapes
- Melons
- Peaches
- Plums
- Raspberries

August Sale Items:
- Back-to-school stationery items
- Juice boxes
- Lunch box products

September Seasonal Produce:
- Artichokes
- Beans
- Cucumbers
- Eggplant
- Peppers
- Squash

- Tomatoes
- Apples
- Oranges
- Pears
- Pomegranates

September Sale Items:
- Bread
- Diabetic food products
- Lunch box products
- Tomato products

October Seasonal Produce:
- Arugula
- Beets
- Broccoli
- Brussels sprouts
- Cabbage
- Kale
- Parsnips
- Potatoes
- Pumpkins
- Spinach
- Squash
- Turnips

- Yams
- Apples
- Cranberries
- Kumquats
- Lemons
- Pomegranates
- Chestnuts

October Sale Items:
- Baking products
- Candy
- Cookies
- Nuts

November Seasonal Produce:
- Beets
- Bok choy
- Broccoli
- Brussels sprouts
- Cabbage
- Carrots
- Celery
- Chard
- Kale
- Leeks

- Mustard greens
- Parsnips
- Potatoes
- Sweet potatoes
- Turnips
- Winter squash
- Yams
- Cranberries
- Kiwi
- Lemons
- Oranges
- Pears

November Sale Items:
- Baking supplies
- Broths
- Canned pumpkin
- Coffee
- Stuffing
- Tea
- Turkey

December Seasonal Produce:

- Bok choy
- Broccoli
- Brussels sprouts
- Carrots
- Cauliflower
- Celery
- Kale
- Red cabbage
- Savoy cabbage
- Spinach
- Sweet potatoes
- White potatoes
- Winter squash
- Yams
- Dates
- Grapefruit
- Hass avocados
- Kiwi
- Kumquats
- Lemons
- Oranges
- Pears

December Sale Items:

- Baking supplies
- Bread/rolls
- Cream soups
- Eggnog
- Ham
- Party platters
- Pie filling
- Snacks
- Soda
- Sour cream
- Stuffing

You can also see seasonal sales on produce on this page at our website: lrwc.co/GrocerySalesCycles

Your Assignment

THE NEXT TIME YOU prepare for a grocery shopping trip, be sure that you:

1. Read your store's flier and look for items that are on sale.

2. Go through your coupons and match those coupons with the sales.

3. Look for store promotions or store coupons you can match with those coupons.

4. Better yet, head over to LivingRichWithCoupons. com, find your store and use the match-ups already prepared for you.

5. If you like to crunch numbers, make yourself a price book so you can track the best prices on items you buy. I don't use one, but I know that many people like to keep a list of prices handy to refer to.

The simple, seemingly obvious, strategy of waiting to use your coupons until the items drop to their lowest prices and then stocking up on them is what changed my couponing world. It's one of the reasons that my $300-a-week grocery bill dropped to about $50. Wow!

Are you pumped to save? I'm pumped for you! I have so much more to share with you. For instance, do you know if your store takes competitor coupons? If you don't know, let's jump into the next chapter, where we address exactly how to use those coupons to take advantage of all the savings available to you. You'll probably be surprised by the savings opportunities you've been missing out on.

Chapter Seven

How to Use Coupons

REMEMBER THE DAY I found out that some of the stores where I shop allow customers to use a store coupon along with a manufacturer coupon. It was a couponing epiphany! On one hand I was thrilled at this newfound knowledge to save even more money, but on the other, I thought, "Bummer for me—look at all the opportunities to save that I missed all these years."

I don't want you to miss those opportunities like I did. I don't want you to scratch your head and ask, "Why didn't I know that?" So I'm going to help you to uncover every savings opportunity at your local stores. You're going to find out exactly what you need to do to save and how to use those coupons correctly.

Remember when I said that in the beginning, couponing is like starting a new job? At your new job you usually get some sort of company orientation manual, procedures manual, or company policy to look over. These usually cover things like how to log into the company's website, what's expected of your position, when you get paid, forms you have to fill out, and things you can and cannot do during working hours. Well, think of the store coupon policies as your work manual.

The coupon policy will teach you what you can and cannot do while using coupons in each store, and it will tell you about other savings opportunities you can take advantage of. I've included store policies in the appendix to give you an idea of what you can expect. But policies often change, so be sure to find your store's current policy and read it carefully. Most stores have their coupon policies on their websites. If you have trouble finding one, head over to LivingRichWithCoupons.com and click on "Find My Store." Locate your store and select the coupon policy for that store. Print it out so you have it handy until you've learned what you need to know.

Here are some of the points you should be checking out in your store's coupon policy:

- Does it accept competitor coupons? If so, does it allow coupons only from certain local stores or national stores? Are there restrictions on when it accepts competitor coupons? Some stores will take a competitor coupon but it must have a dollar amount listed on the coupon. For instance, they'll take a coupon for $1 off a loaf of bread, but they won't take the coupon for 20 percent off a loaf of bread.

- Does it double coupons? If so, what's the policy on doubling coupons? Does it have a limit per day? What coupon values double? For instance, does a $1 coupon double, or is it just coupons valued at $0.99 or less?
- Can you stack a store coupon with a manufacturer coupon?
- What is its policy on using coupons with a BOGO sale? Can you use a coupon on the product you're getting free from the sale?
- Does it offer eCoupons or other discounts you can take advantage of? If so, what is its policy on using eCoupons?
- Does it offer price-matching? If so, what's the policy on price-matching? Do you need the competitor's ad to prove the price? Does your store match online pricing?
- Does it have a limit on the number of coupons you may use per transaction and/or per product? If so, what is that limit?

- Does it have a policy regarding coupons that don't scan? Some stores will not accept coupons if they don't scan.
- What is the store's policy for coupons whose value is higher than the product price? Does it give overage or does it reduce the price of the coupon to the sale price of the product?

As you can see, some of these policies could be game-changers for shopping at the store, and there may be some stores you decide to stop patronizing.

Whatever the case, if you're fully aware of a store's policy, it makes it so much easier to shop confidently, knowing you're following its policy and knowing what to expect when you check out. If you have six of the same coupons for boxed macaroni and cheese and you put six boxes in your cart, you'll have an unpleasant surprise waiting when you check out if the store limits same coupons to four per shopping trip. So make sure you're prepared by reading and understanding the coupon policies for your stores. If you don't understand something in a policy, stop by your customer service counter and ask for clarification. I've done that numerous times at many stores. I've even contacted customer service via e-mail or phone to get a better understanding of what policies mean. Knowledge is power!

The best coupon policy that I discovered is one that allows you to use a coupon on a free item when drugstores have a BOGO sale. One of the best deals is when the store has a BOGO sale and you have a BOGO coupon for the same product. It turns out that you can use that coupon to score two free products. (CVS is currently the only drugstore that allows this.) It took me years to find this out. Yes indeed, buy two products, get one free and use a BOGO coupon and get both free. How cool is that? It's that easy! See the importance of knowing your coupon policies and knowing exactly how to use those coupons? So go on—empower yourself with the knowledge of how to use coupons at your local stores.

Once you read and understand your store's coupon policies, you'll be ready to head into the next and probably most important step of couponing, which is learning how and why you should stock up. You've been empowered with knowledge regarding where to get your coupons and when and how to use them. The next step is to empower yourself with control, and your stockpile will give you that control.

Chapter Eight

Stock Up and Save

Stockpile, noun: *a large supply of food gathered and held in reserve for use during a shortage or during a period of higher prices.*

Stockpile, verb: *to accumulate for future use; put or store in a stockpile.*

TALK TO ANY COUPONER and you'll soon find out that they're proud of their stockpile. And why not? They *should* be proud. I know I was when I first started couponing, and I still am to this day. But why exactly does that stockpile make a couponer so proud?

• • •

IF YOU'VE EVER WATCHED any of the couponing shows on television—you know, the ones where living rooms have been turned into mini-markets—then you're probably saying to yourself, "Oh, here she goes, getting all extreme on me. I knew there had to be a catch. I am not going to start hoarding groceries." Don't go there. That's *not* what I'm talking about. I'm talking about the great results that real people get from stockpiling.

For example, Lisa, a single mother with five children, has learned to save a bundle by couponing and maintaining a stockpile. She had always used coupons, mainly at grocery stores, but she got serious about couponing when her youngest daughter was headed off to college. "I was newly separated and struggling trying to find ways to save money anywhere I could," she said. "I became a member of Living Rich With Coupons, and reading all the match-up posts showed me how easy it could be to reduce my costs on everyday items."

Knowing that her daughter would need personal-hygiene items, laundry detergent, cooking supplies, paper products, cleaning supplies, and other household items for her apartment, Lisa made a list and then used the LivingRichWithCoupons.com weekly match-ups and coupon-stacking to start a small stockpile. "My very first real couponing trip was to CVS for personal care products," she said. "The register rang up at $103, but by the time my ECBs and coupons and store savings were applied, my total turned into $29.87. I was hooked! Thank you for starting your website. You have truly been a blessing in sharing your knowledge with those of us who need every little bit of help we can get."

By the time Lisa's daughter left for college, she had stockpiled enough for her entire first year of apartment living, and there was plenty for all four roommates to share! "I've also got my own stockpile," Lisa said, "and with a sixteen-year-old son, that definitely comes in handy." Her space is limited, so she stockpiles items like toilet paper, paper towels, detergent, and cleaning products since they're often the most expensive items.

Couponers are proud of their stockpiles for good reason! This small supply of food, household supplies, and health and beauty aids should last you eight to twelve weeks because sales cycles run about every eight to twelve weeks. If you've found an awesome sale on a product that your family uses, make sure to buy enough to last you about three months. Remember, a stockpile is "held in reserve" for use "during a period of higher prices." This is where you, as a couponer, gain control over your grocery spending. Let's use the same example we used in Chapter Six to see how stocking up gives you control.

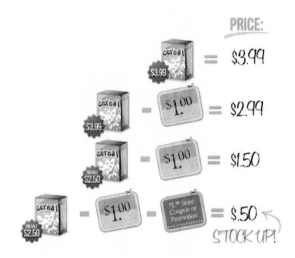

Let's say your family eats this particular brand of cereal, and with a family of four you go through about a box a week. A good stock-up amount for you would be about twelve boxes of cereal to cover a twelve-week period. But let's say it's on sale and you buy only two boxes. After two weeks, what happens? Yep, you'll need to buy more cereal. This time, however, it's not on sale, so you're forced to pay $3.99 for another box and keep your fingers crossed that it will be on sale again the next week. Chances are it won't be, considering that cycles run around every two to three months. So for the next few weeks you're forced to buy the cereal for $3.99 a box or not buy it at all.

Now let's back up to three weeks ago when it was on sale at a stock-up price. You pick up twelve boxes and place them in your stockpile. You are now in control of how much you pay for that box of cereal. Why? Because you can wait. You can wait until the next great sale and you aren't forced to pay that higher price to feed your family. This control over the price you'll pay for products is the most empowering part of couponing!

Stockpiling Isn't Just for Couponers

STOCKING UP AT THE lowest prices is a good idea whether you have coupons for the product or not. Yes, using coupons will reduce your grocery costs even more, but let's say you can't get twelve coupons for those boxes of cereals that are on sale. That doesn't mean you should let that great sale get away. Stocking up at $2.50 a box is much better than paying $4 a box in the coming weeks. So don't shy away from stocking up just because you don't have enough coupons.

It Takes Time to See the Savings

WHEN I GIVE COUPONING workshops, the thing I stress the most is that you won't start saving thousands of dollars on day one. It's a process, and it will take some time to build your stockpile in order to start seeing a drop in your grocery bill.

The week I started couponing, I had no stockpile. All I had were the items in my pantry, which probably consisted of a few boxes of cereal, rice, a few snacks, cans of tuna, and cans of tomatoes and other vegetables. My freezer had a few bags of frozen veggies, a tub of ice cream, and some mystery items that I didn't even remember putting in there. So I was really starting from scratch.

I started shopping at CVS the first week and scored a couple of free tubes of toothpaste and a couple of bottles of shampoo. My stockpile was born! Stocking up on some toothpaste and shampoo certainly didn't reduce my grocery bill by that much, but it was a start.

In week two, I found myself stocking up on more toothpaste, more shampoo, deodorant, and window cleaner. In week three, I stocked up on body wash, peanut butter, and more deodorant. In week four, I broadened my shopping to my local grocery store, stocking up on cereal, barbecue sauce, and eggs.

After week four of couponing and stocking up, my grocery list started getting smaller and I started getting picky about the prices I would pay for certain items because I had control on some of the items I had already stocked up on. I noticed my grocery bill drop from $300 a week to $200 a week after just four weeks. After eight weeks, the bill was down to $100 a week.

After twelve weeks, I had built up such a nice stockpile of groceries that all I was spending was about $50 a week on milk, produce, and meat. It was the most empowering feeling in the world knowing that I had so much control over my spending.

Eventually, there were times when I could skip a week or two of grocery shopping altogether, living completely off my stockpile. That's the biggest money- and time-saver of all.

I'm not going to lie to you. The beginning was hard. Remember, like when you start a new job, you have to get organized, learn all the rules, and learn how to do your "job" correctly. What will wind up taking you thirty minutes a week after a few months will take you three hours in the beginning. But I promise you, it gets easier. And remember, there are weeks you won't have to coupon at all. I know a lot of people who coupon all fall, winter, and spring and take the summer off. I tend to do that myself as well, but I always jump on any great deals that are available during the summer months.

Don't Limit Your Stockpile to Shelf-Stable Items

STOCKING UP ISN'T LIMITED to shelf-stable products, household products, or health and beauty aids. There are many dairy products, produce, and meats you can stock up on as well.

For instance, I'm a big fan of manager-special meats. I have figured out when the meat department at my local store marks down its meats and try to make a trip to the store around that time. These mark downs are made when the expiration date of the meats is fast approaching. Most times I'll freeze the meat right away, so it doesn't matter that the sell-by date is that day or the next day. If you don't know when they mark down meat in your store, be sure to ask your meat manager. Same goes for the bakery department.

I've picked up turkey burgers for as little as $0.29 for a four-pack with manager-special coupons attached to them. One day they had eight-packs of the turkey available and I picked up thirty-two burgers for just $2.32—less than the cost of *one package*. I couldn't stop myself from breaking into my happy dance!

And did you know you can freeze milk? Yep, just remove a little from the container so there's room for the milk to expand, and put it in the freezer. You can freeze eggs, too. Don't scrunch your eyebrows thinking I'm crazy—you really can. Simply crack each egg into one section of an ice-cube tray, use a fork to mix up the yolk and the white, put it in the freezer to set and then put them in a freezer bag. They'll be there the next time you want to make an omelet or scrambled eggs, or you need them for baking. So next time you see eggs at an awesome price, stock up and freeze them!

Small-Space Stockpiling

I KNOW THAT FOR some of you, space could be an issue when building your stockpile. If you don't have enough room to keep a nicely sized stockpile, no worries—just keep it small. Choose the items that are most important to you and your family and stock up on those. For instance, my daughter lives in a small apartment, and she keeps baskets in her linen closet for health and beauty products like free toothpaste, deodorant, and shampoo. This saves her a lot of money on those items without taking up too much space. Bulkier items like toilet paper and paper towels, when scored at a great price, can be stored under a bed. Be creative with the space you have. In most cases, if you get a little more organized, you can create enough free space for a good stockpile.

Food Storage Guidelines

Food	Pantry (Room Temperature)	Refrigerator (33°F to 40°F)	Freezer (32°F)
Bread and Cereal Products			
Baked quick breads	4-5 days	1-2 weeks	2-3 months
Bread	5-7 days	1-2 weeks	2-3 months
Bread crumbs and croutons	6 months		
Bread rolls, unbaked		2-3 weeks	1 month
Cereals, ready-to-eat	1 year		
	2-3 months*		
Cereals, ready-to-cook	6 months		
Corn meal	1 year	18 months	2 years
Doughnuts	4-5 days		3 months
Flour, all-purpose, white	6-8 months	1 year	1-2 years
Flour, whole wheat		6-8 months	1-2 years
Pasta	2 years		
Pies and pastries		3 days	4-6 months
Pies and pastries, baked			1-2 months
Pies and pastries, cream filled		2-3 days	3 months
Pizza		3-4 days	1-2 months
Rice, brown	6 months		
Rice, white	1 year	6-7 days+	6 months+
Tacos, enchiladas, and burritos (frozen)		2 weeks	1 year
Waffles		4-5 days	1 month
Packaged Foods and Mixes			
Biscuit, brownie, and muffin mixes	9 months		
Cakes, prepared	2-4 days		2-3 months
Cake mixes	6-9 months		
Casserole mix	9-12 months		
Chili powder	6 months		
Cookies, packaged	2 months		8-12 months
Crackers, pretzels	3 months		
Frosting, canned	3 months		
Frosting, mix	8 months		
Fruit cake		2-3 months	1 year
Hot roll mix	18 months		
Instant breakfast products	6 months		
Pancake and piecrust mix	6 months		
Pancake waffle batter		1-2 days	3 months
Toaster pastries	3 months		
Sauce and gravy mixes	6 months		
Soup mixes	1 year		

* Opened   + Cooked   ^ Refrigerate after opening   # After manufacture date

Food	Pantry (Room Temperature)	Refrigerator (33°F to 40°F)	Freezer (32°F)
Spices, Herbs, Condiments, Extracts			
Catsup, chili, and cocktail sauce	1 year		
	1 month*	6 months	
Herbs	6 months		1-2 years
Herb/spice blends	2 years		1-2 years
	1 year *		
Mustard	2 years	6-8 months*	8-12 months
Spices, ground	6 months		1-2 years
Spices, whole	1-2 years		2-3 years
Vanilla extract	2 years		
	1 year*		
Other extracts	1 year		
Other Food Staples			
Bacon bits	4 months		
Baking powder	18 months		
Baking soda	2 years		
Bouillon products	1 year		
Carbonated soft drinks (12 oz. cans)	6-9 months		
Carbonated soft drinks, diet (12 oz. cans)	3-4 months		
Chocolate, premelted	1 year		
Chocolate syrup	2 years	6 months*	
Chocolate, semisweet	2 years		
Chocolate, unsweetened	18 months		
Cocoa mixes	8 months		
Coconut, shredded	1 year		
	6 months*	8 months	1 year
Coffee cans	2 years		
	2 weeks*	2 months	6 months
Coffee, instant	6 months		
	2 weeks*		
Coffee, vacuum-packed	1 year ^		
Coffee lighteners (dry)	9 months		1 year
	6 months*		
Cornstarch	18 months		2 years
Gelatin	18 months		
Honey, jams, jellies, and syrup	1 year	6-8 months*	
Marshmallows	2-3 months		
Marshmallow cream	3-4 months		
Mayonnaise	2-3 months	12 months	
		2 months*	
Molasses	2 years		
Nuts, shelled	4 months	6 months	
Nuts, unshelled	6 months		
Nuts, salted			6-8 months

Food	Pantry (Room Temperature)	Refrigerator (33°F to 40°F)	Freezer (32°F)
Other Food Staples (continued)			
Nuts, unsalted			9-12 months
Oil, salad	3 months^		
	2 months*		
Parmesan grated cheese	10 months		
	2 months*		
Pasteurized process cheese spread	3 months	3-4 weeks*	4 months
Peanut butter	6-9 months	4-6 months	
	2-3 months*		
Popcorn	1-2 years	2 years	2-3 years
Pectin	1 year		
Salad dressings, bottled	1 year^	3 months*	
Soft drinks	3 months		
Artificial sweetener	2 years		
Sugar, brown	4 months		
Sugar, confectioners	18 months		
Sugar, granulated	2 years		
Tea bags	18 months		
Tea, instant	2 years		
Vegetable oils	6 months		
	1-3 months*		
Vegetable shortening	3 months	6-9 months	
Vinegar	2 years		
	1 year*		
Water, bottled	1-2 years		
Whipped topping (dry)	1 year		
Yeast, dry	Pkg. exp. date		
Vegetables			
Asparagus		2-3 days	8 months
Beets		2 weeks	
Broccoli		3-5 days	
Brussels sprouts		3-5 days	
Cabbage		1 week	
Carrots		2 weeks	
Cauliflower		1 week	
Celery		1 week	
Corn (husks)		1-2 days	8 months
Cucumbers		1 week	
Eggplant		1 week	
Green beans		1-2 days	8 months
Green peas		3-5 days	8 months
Lettuce		1 week	
Lima beans		3-5 days	8 months
Mushrooms		2 days	
Onions	1 week	3-5 days	

Food	Pantry (Room Temperature)	Refrigerator (33°F to 40°F)	Freezer (32°F)
Vegetables (continued)			
Onion rings (precooked, frozen)			1 year#
Peppers		1 week	
Pickles, canned	1 year	1 month*	
Frozen potatoes			8 month
Sweet potatoes	2-3 weeks		
White potatoes	2-3 months		
Potato chips	1 month		
Radishes		2 weeks	
Rhubarb		3-5 days	
Rutabagas	1 week		
Snap beans		1 week	
Spinach		5-7 days	8 months
Squash, Summer		3-5 days	
Squash, Winter	1 week		
Tomatoes		1 week	
Turnips		2 weeks	
Commercial baby food, jars	1-2 years^	2-3 days	
Canned vegetables	1 year^	3-5 days*	
Canned vegetables, pickled	1 year^	1-2 months*	
Dried vegetables	6 months		
Frozen vegetables			8 months
Vegetable soup		3-4 days	3 months
Fruits			
Apples	Until ripe	1 month	
Apricots	Until ripe	5 days	
Avocados	Until ripe	5 days	
Bananas	Until ripe	5 days (fully ripe)	
Berries	Until ripe	3 days	1 year
Canned fruit	1 year	2-4 days*	
Canned fruit juices	1 year	3-5 days*	
Cherries	Until ripe	3 days	
Citrus fruit	Until ripe	2 weeks	
Dried fruit	6 months	2-4 days+	
Frozen fruit			1 year
Fruit juice concentrate		6 days	1 year
Fruit pies, baked		2-3 days	8 months
Fruit, pre-cut, fresh	Until ripe	2-4 days	1 year
Grapes	Until ripe	5 days	
Melons	Until ripe	5 days	
Nectarines	Until ripe	5 days	
Peaches	Until ripe	5 days	1 year
Pears	Until ripe	5 days	1 year
Pineapple	Until ripe	5-7 days	1 year
Plums	Until ripe	5 days	

Food	Pantry (Room Temperature)	Refrigerator (33°F to 40°F)	Freezer (32°F)
Dairy Products			
Butter		1-2 months	9 months
Buttermilk		2 weeks	
Cottage cheese		1 week	3 months
Cream cheese		2 weeks	
Cream-light, heavy, half- and-half		3-4 days	1-4 months
Eggnog commercial		3-5 days	6 months
Margarine		4-5 months	12 months
Condensed, evaporated and dry milk	12-23 months^	8-20 days*	
Milk		8-20 days	3 months
Ice cream and sherbet			2 months
Hard natural cheese (e.g. cheddar, swiss)		3-6 months 3-4 weeks*	6 months
Processed cheese		3-4 weeks	6-8 months
Soft cheese (e.g. brie)		1 week	6 months
Pudding		1-2 days*	
Snack dips		1 week*	
Sour cream		2 weeks	
Non-dairy whipped cream, canned		3 months	
Real whipped cream, canned		3-4 weeks	
Yogurt		2 weeks	1-2 months
MEATS, FISH, POULTRY, AND EGGS			
Meats			
Fresh beef and bison steaks		3-5 days	6-9 months
Fresh beef and bison roasts		3-5 days	9-12 months
Fresh pork chops		3-5 days	4-6 months
Fresh lamb chops		3-5 days	6-8 months
Fresh veal		1-2 days	4-6 months
Fresh ground meat (e.g. beef, bison, veal, lamb)		1-2 days	3-4 months
Cooked meat		2-3 days	2-3 months
Canned meat	1 year	3-4 days*	3-4 months
Ham, whole		1 week	1-2 months
Ham, canned	2 years	1 week*	3-4 months
Ham, canned "keep refrigerated"		6-9 months 3-5 days*	3-4 months
Shelf-stable unopened canned meat (e.g. chili, deviled ham, corn beef)	1 year	1week*	
Ham, cook before eating		1 week	
Ham, fully cooked		2 weeks 1 week*	
Ham, dry-cured	1 year	1 month	
Ham salad, store prepared or homemade		3-5 days	
Bacon		2 weeks 1 week*	1 month
Corned beef, uncooked		5-7 days	1-2 months

Food	Pantry (Room Temperature)	Refrigerator (33°F to 40°F)	Freezer (32°F)
Meats (continued)			
Restructured (flaked) meat products			9-12 months
Sausage, fresh		1-2 days	1-2 months
Smoked breakfast sausage links, patties		1 week	2 months
Sausage, smoked (e.g. Mettwurst)		1 week	1-2 months
Sausage, semi-dry (e.g. Summer sausage)		2-3 weeks*	6 months
Sausage, dry smoked (e.g. Pepperoni, jerky, dry Salami)	1 year	1 month*	6 months
Frankfurters, bologna		2 weeks 3-7 days*	1-2 months
Luncheon meat		2 weeks 3-7 days*	1-2 months
Meat gravies		1-2 days	2-3 months
TV beef and pork dinners			18 months#
Meat based casseroles		3-4 days	4 months
Variety meats (giblets. tongue, liver, heart, etc.)		1-2 days	3-4 months
Vinegar pickled meats (e.g. pickled pigs feet)	1 year^	2 weeks*	
Fish			
Breaded fish			4-6 months
Canned fish	1 year	1-2 days*	
Cooked fish or seafood		3-4 days	3 months
Lean fish (e.g. cod, flounder, haddock)		1-2 days	6-10 months
Fatty fish (e.g. bluefish, salmon, mackeral)		1-2 days	2-3 months
Dry pickled fish		3-4 weeks	
Smoked fish		2 weeks	4-5 weeks
Seafood-clams, crab, lobster in shell		2 days	3 months
Seafood-oysters and scallops		4-5 days	3-4 months
Seafood-shrimp		4-5 days	3 months
Seafood-shucked clams		4-5 days	3 months
Tuna salad, store prepared or homemade		3-5 days	
Poultry			
Chicken nuggets or patties		1-2 days	
Chicken livers		1-2 days	3 months
Chicken and poultry TV dinners			6 months
Canned poultry^	2-5 years	3-4 days*	4-6 weeks
Cooked poultry		2-3 days	4-6 months
Fresh poultry		1-2 days	1 year
Frozen poultry parts		1-2 days	6-9 months
Canned poultry		1 day	3 months
Poultry pies, stews, and gravies		1-2 days	6 months
Poultry salads, store prepared or homemade		3-5 days	
Poultry stuffing, cooked		3-4 days	1 month

Food	Pantry (Room Temperature)	Refrigerator (33°F to 40°F)	Freezer (32°F)
Eggs			
Eggs, in shell		3-5 weeks	
Eggs, hard-boiled		1 week	
Eggs, pasteurized, liquid		10 days	1 year
		3 days*	
Egg substitute		10 days	1 year
		3 days*	
Egg yolks (covered in water)		2-4 days	1 year
Egg whites		2-4 days	1 year
(For each cup of egg yolk add			
1 Tbs. of sugar or salt)			
Wild Game			
Frog legs		1 day	6-9 months
Game birds		2 days	9 months
Small game (rabbit, squirrel, etc.)		2 days	9-12 months
Venison ground meat		1-2 days	2-3 months
Venison steaks and roasts		3-5 days	9-12 months

Virginia Cooperative Extension publication #348-960

Most herbs and spices are cheaper fresh than dry, so we buy rosemary, thyme, oregano, and some others fresh and then dry them and put them in jars. You can also freeze your fresh herbs. To do that, simply chop them and place them in ice cube trays. Add olive oil to the tray, leaving room at the top for expansion. Place the trays in the freezer until the herbs are frozen. When they are, pop them out of the ice cube tray and place them in a Ziploc bag for future use.

A great book for learning more about freezing and canning is *Preserving Summer's Bounty: A Quick and Easy Guide to Freezing, Canning, Preserving, and Drying What You Grow*, by the Rodale Food Center and Susan McClure.

Of course, having an extra freezer has made all this freezing even easier, but freezers can be expensive. We got our freezer at a "scratch and dent" facility. The scratches are barely noticeable, the freezer works perfectly, and we saved quite a bit of money. Some other ways to score yourself a freezer for a great price are to check grocery stores during March, which is National Frozen Foods Month. There are always tons of great sales on freezer foods then, and some stores will tie in a chest freezer with a sale. I've seen them on sale, and when you buy one you get coupons for free food products valued at almost as much as the freezer. Of course, there are always Black Friday sales to watch for, too.

Now that you've learned where to get your coupons, when and how to use them, and how to stock up, in the next chapter you'll learn how you can buy healthy and even organic products without breaking the bank! This is one of my favorite topics, so get ready for some big surprises!

Chapter Nine

Eat Healthy With Coupons!

A T LEAST ONCE A week I meet someone who says they don't use coupons because they're only for processed foods. The truth is, there are coupons for fruits, veggies, dairy, meat, and organic foods. But even without those coupons, you can save a ton on household items like toilet paper, laundry detergent, shampoo, and toothpaste. Saving money on cleaning supplies, cosmetics, vitamins, and other non-food items can free up extra cash to spend on the things that are important to you and your family. You really can save money and eat healthy on a budget! Besides the coupons available for healthier options, there are many other ways to save and eat healthily.

Freeze Produce When It's in Season

ZERO IN ON THE produce that's in season in your area. For instance, in New Jersey where I live, strawberries are in peak season in early June. That's the time I can pick them up at the lowest price, so I stock up on them, enjoy them in recipes and by themselves, and freeze a bunch for the off-seasons, when prices are higher.

Make Simple Recipes With Basic Ingredients

I USED TO THINK I had to cook with fancy ingredients to make a healthy meal. While kelp noodles might be nice to add to a stir-fry, they're not something I use regularly. I use them for one or two recipes and they sit in my cabinet until I throw them away. That's a waste of money. Sticking with basic ingredients makes it easier to get a grasp on prices so you know when you've found a great deal and should stock up.

Here are some basic healthy ingredients to stock up on:

- Raw nuts and seeds
- Whole grains like rice, quinoa, amaranth, and millet
- Rolled and steel-cut oats
- Cold-pressed oils: almond, coconut, macadamia nut, olive, sunflower seed, walnut, etc.
- Coconut palm sugar
- Medjool dates
- Pure maple syrup
- Local raw honey

- Nut milks (almond or coconut)
- Sweet potatoes, squash, and yams
- Fresh ginger root
- Dried beans

Here are additional items you may want to stock up on:
- Gluten-free flours like almond, quinoa, and rice
- Flax seed and/or meal
- Kale (freeze leaves for use in soups, or juice it and freeze the juice)
- Balsamic vinegar
- Apple cider vinegar
- Bananas (slice and freeze, or freeze in the skin)

A great resource for finding delicious, healthy recipes is www.mywholefoodlife.com. The recipes stick with most of these simple, basic ingredients, which is a big money-saver when you're trying to eat healthily and save money on your groceries.

Be Selective

BUYING ONLY ORGANIC FOODS can be very expensive. If you can afford to do that, great, but you can save money by buying only the fruits and vegetables that are considered to be highest in pesticides.

The Environmental Working Group has analyzed testing data from the US Department of Agriculture and the Food and Drug Administration and come up with rankings for produce that's most important to buy organic and produce that's clean enough that we don't need to buy organic. The fruits and veggies with the least amount of pesticide residue are included in the Clean Fifteen, and the foods with the most pesticide residue are listed in the Dirty Dozen.

The list changes each year, so bookmark EWG for the latest lists: www.ewg.org/foodnews/list.php

Dirty Dozen
(those with the most pesticide residue)

1. Apples

2. Strawberries

3. Grapes

4. Celery

5. Peaches

6. Spinach

7. Sweet bell peppers

8. Imported nectarines

9. Cucumbers

10. Cherry tomatoes

11. Imported snap peas

12. Potatoes

Clean Fifteen
(those with the least amount of pesticide residue)

1. Avocados

2. Sweet corn

3. Pineapple

4. Cabbage

5. Sweet peas—frozen

6. Onions

7. Asparagus

8. Mangoes

9. Papaya

10. Kiwi

11. Eggplant

12. Grapefruit

13. Cantaloupe

14. Cauliflower

15. Sweet potatoes

Finding Coupons for Healthier Options

Coupons for organic produce, dairy products, and meat are available online through coupon websites like Coupons.com, but you can also find them on sites dedicated to healthier options. Those sites include MamboSprouts.com and CommonKindness.com. Other sites such as Snap by Groupon, BerryCart, Checkout 51, Ibotta, and SavingStar often have rebate offers for produce, dairy, and meat products. Also, stores like Whole Foods have their own store coupons available that can be combined with manufacturer coupons for even more savings.

Signing up for brand newsletters and liking companies' Facebook pages is another way to be alerted of coupons for the healthier products that you use most often. You can also contact the company directly and ask if it provides coupons that can be mailed to you. More often than not, you'll find that brands are willing to mail you out a few coupons for their products.

Seek Out Alternative Options

Knowing the price points for the products you use the most is important, so keeping your ingredients to a minimum can help you to avoid being overwhelmed with trying to remember prices.

Another big money-saver is keeping your options open regarding where you shop. For instance, I'd been paying $7.99 for two pounds of Medjool dates, which comes to about $4 a pound. I then spotted a three-pound pack of Medjool dates for just $8.99, or about $3 a pound. Of course, I jumped on that deal. I've found chia seeds, organic granola, flax seed, and more at my local HomeGoods store at much lower prices than at some of the organic stores.

You can also look into a food cooperative in your area. Food co-ops are worker- or customer-owned businesses that provide grocery items of the highest quality and best value to their members (source: www.localharvest.org/food-coops/). There's also the community-supported agriculture movement. CSAs are a way for you to buy local produce in season directly from a farmer. Customers buy "shares" from farmers and receive a box of seasonal produce every week through the farming season (source: www.localharvest.org/csa/).

Grow Your Own

IF YOU HAVEN'T DONE so before, consider trying your hand at gardening. There's nothing better than picking and eating your own homegrown produce. It's a lot less expensive than buying at the grocery store.

If you're new to gardening, don't go crazy right away. Choose easy-to-grow items like tomatoes, lettuce, peppers, and beans. Once you get the hang of it, you can expand your selection.

Reduce Your Meat

A HEALTHY WAY TO cut the cost of your groceries is to reduce your meat consumption. Substituting beans is a nutritious, inexpensive way to make a meal filling. Beans are high in fiber, low in fat, and have five to seven grams of protein per cup.

The healthiest and least expensive option is to buy beans dried instead of canned. When using dried beans, be sure to rinse and soak them overnight before cooking. You can also cook beans and freeze them.

Here are some suggestions for using beans in place of meat:

- Use them in a meatless chili.

- Make "hamburgers" by combining cooked beans, onions, garlic, eggs, bread crumbs, and seasoning in a food processor. Form the mixture into patties and grill as usual.
- Add beans to a quinoa salad for a healthy one-dish meal. Cook the quinoa, add the cooked beans, peppers, onions, corn, or any veggies you have in your fridge. Toss with apple cider vinegar and olive oil for a delicious alternative meal.
- Make bean burritos or tacos by mashing black beans and mixing them with salsa in soft- or hard-shell tacos with lettuce and cheese.

As you can see, your options for eating healthily on a budget are endless.

Part Three

*Save More,
Live Richer!*

Chapter Ten

Step Up Your Savings

ONCE YOU'VE GOTTEN COMFORTABLE with what you learned in Part Two, you can step up your savings by layering even more offers and deals. By taking advantaging of these extra offers and continuing to stock up, you can lower your grocery bill even more.

Chances are you've heard of some of these techniques but may not have used them to take advantage of all your savings opportunities. So, without further ado, let's get into even more ways for you to save.

Rebates

THERE ARE TONS OF rebates out there, in many shapes and forms. Some rebates print out on your grocery store receipt, making it easy to fill out the form and submit it. Some rebates are available on brands' websites or Facebook pages. Some are on a peelie or hang tag located right on the product.

In this digital age, we have tons of new rebates available in the form of apps. These apps, available for your smartphone or tablets, are easy to use, making savings a snap. As a matter of fact, one of the rebate apps is called just that—Snap.

To take advantage of these rebates you simply have to take a photo of your receipt showing your qualifying purchase. Once the company verifies your purchase, you get your money for the rebate deposited into your account. Pretty easy, right?!

Some of the apps are:

- Snap by Groupon
- Ibotta
- Berry Cart
- Checkout 51
- MobiSave

Most rebates allow you to use a coupon on the product, and the end result is that you pay very little or nothing on the product and still get money back. Recently, I had a great opportunity with a battery rebate. The rebate was for $8 via PayPal or check for each pack of the batteries I bought. I simply had to add a code found on the package to a form on the company's website and within four to six weeks it deposited the money into my PayPal account. The great part was that the products were on sale and I had a coupon, making them only $0.49 a pack. And you were allowed to do the rebate eight times. That's a profit of $60!

Deals that good don't come around that often, but there are plenty of times where a sale, a coupon, and a rebate will get you the product for free or even provide you with a profit.

Catalina Deals

CATALINA DEALS OR OFFERS are one of my favorite ways to save even more. They are coupons that print out of the Catalina machine at participating stores. These machines are usually located next to the register.

Catalina deals require that a certain dollar amount be spent or that a certain quantity of products be purchased, usually in one transaction. Once you've met the qualifications, a Catalina coupon for a certain amount off your next purchase will be printed. Usually, it can be applied toward anything in the store, though some promotions require that they be used toward a specific brand or product.

Here's an example of a Catalina that requires you to purchase a certain amount of products: "Buy five participating name-brand products and get a $5 Catalina." This simply means that you need to purchase five of the items listed in the promotion and you'll receive a $5 Catalina coupon that you can use on your next purchase.

Here's an example of a Catalina that requires you to spend a certain dollar amount: "Buy $25 worth of name-brand products and get a $5 Catalina." This type of Catalina requires you to spend $25 on participating products. When you do, you'll receive a $5 Catalina that you can use on your next purchase.

In most cases you can use coupons on the products included in the offer and reduce your out-of-pocket expense, making these store promotions even better.

Drugstore Deals

THREE OF THE MAJOR drugstore chains have great rewards programs that are similar to Catalina offers. Each of these stores requires you to sign up for its free store loyalty card in order to get the rewards.

CVS – ExtraCare Rewards Program

Like Catalina Deals, these rewards print out once you've met the qualifying purchases. Those qualifications may be met by buying a specific quantity of select products or spending a certain dollar amount. The only difference with the ExtraCare Rewards is that they print at the end of your receipt instead of on a separate coupon like Catalina offers.

Walgreens – Register Rewards

Walgreens' Register Rewards offer the same type of deals as CVS ExtraCare Rewards and Catalina coupons. The rewards are printed separately from your receipt.

Walgreens also has the Balance Rewards Points program. The program requires you to have a Balance Rewards loyalty card. By signing up and using the loyalty card, you can earn points each week for select products. Look for the Balance Rewards symbol in your weekly ad.

These points will accumulate on your Balance Rewards card and you can redeem as few as 5,000 Balance Rewards points at a time. Points expire thirty-six months from the time you earn them.

Rain Checks

YEARS AGO, I DIDN'T give rain checks any thought. I couldn't be bothered with going to customer service and getting those little pieces of paper that I would usually misplace anyway. That was until I learned the true value of a rain check.

Rain checks are a great way to take advantage of deals when the products are no longer in stock. Sometimes you can even score a better deal than the one that was originally available.

A great way to take advantage of a rain check is to use it when the store is running a promotion, especially if the price of the rain check is better than the price of the item in the deal for that week.

Here are some tips to help you save with rain checks:

1. Know Your Store's Rain Check Policy

HERE ARE THREE QUESTIONS to ask your store about rain checks:

1. Is there a limit on the amount of products I can purchase with the rain check?

2. If the product was part of another deal, will I still be able to take advantage of that deal when I use my rain check?

3. Do the rain checks have expiration dates?

2. Combine CVS Rain Checks With ExtraCare Bucks

IF THE PRODUCT ON sale is not available during the dates of the advertised promotion and it's part of an ExtraCare Bucks cash-back deal, CVS will honor the ExtraCare Bucks at the time you make the purchase. Keep in mind that if an ExtraCare Bucks deal is currently running on the product you're using your rain check on, you'll receive the ExtraCare Bucks only for the current promotion. You won't receive them for the rain check *and* the current promotion.

3. Use Coupons With Rain Checks

YOU CAN USE COUPONS with rain checks. It's no different from using them when the product was on sale originally. So if you didn't have a coupon when the product went on sale and a coupon becomes available later, you can score a great deal by using your rain check at that time.

4. Get Rain Checks for a Product in a Catalina Deal

UNFORTUNATELY, ONCE A CATALINA deal is over, the Catalina machine won't give you a coupon when you use your rain check. You can certainly discuss the deal and the situation with your store's customer service department to see if it will honor the Catalina deal, however.

Price-Matching

WHEN WAS THE LAST time you had a store price-match an item for you? Price-matching is when a store honors the price at a competitor store. Most people don't take advantage of this savings opportunity, and many don't even know it's possible, but several stores have price-matching policies! Not many grocery stores price-match, but Walmart and Target both price-match. So consider heading to your local Walmart or Target if your favorite grocery store is out of the product that's on sale.

Why is price-matching so important? Well, let's say that Pantene Shampoo is on sale this week for only $0.75 a bottle at Walgreens. You have a $1 coupon for Pantene shampoo, but Walgreens' policy states that if the value of the coupon is more than the product, they will not accept the coupon. So, head over to Walmart, which not only allows you to use a coupon on a product that's priced lower than the value of the coupon but even gives you overage for that coupon. That's where price-matching can really benefit you as a couponer!

The following stores guarantee price-matches:

- Amazon
- Best Buy
- Home Depot
- Lowe's
- Nordstrom
- Sears
- Staples
- Target
- Walmart

If you're not sure if your store price-matches, ask at the customer service counter.

Remember, all these policies have exceptions and restrictions, so please be sure to read them carefully before heading out to price-match. Keep in mind that stores can change policies at any time, so it's important to review them from time to time.

Comparing Prices by Unit

FOR MANY YEARS I was under the impression that the bigger the product, the better the deal was going to be, but I was wrong. There are many times when smaller packages are the better deal and may even be a lot better when you throw coupons into the mix.

If you're not using coupons, be sure to look at the unit price of the product.

Unit prices will show how much that product costs based on weight (i.e., per ounce, pound, etc.) or count. You're looking for the lowest unit price for like products. However, that theory gets blown out of the water when you can score a product for free after a coupon.

Here's an example: A one-pound package of Carolina Rice is priced at $1 ($1-per-pound unit price), while a two-pound package is priced at $1.75 ($0.875-per-pound unit price). As you can see, buying the two-pound package would be cheaper, and I would recommend buying the two-pound package *if you don't have any coupons*. But let's say we have a $1/1 coupon that can be used on the one-pound package. After using the coupon, the one-pound package of rice is completely free!

Taking Advantage of Loss Leaders

A LOSS LEADER IS a product that's placed at or below the store's cost to get us in the door. These products are usually at one of their lowest prices during that week, so it's a great time to stock up on them. Usually, loss leaders are meat or produce products, but you can also find loss leaders during holiday months. For instance, November and December are big baking months, and flour may be priced at or below stores' cost for a particular week just to get you in the door to buy the rest of your baking ingredients. The secret is to buy as much as the store allows and stock up at those lower prices. Remember, a three-month supply is a good rule of thumb for the average family.

In the next chapter, I'll explain how to set up a budget. To really live rich, creating a budget is a necessity, and you're about to find out that it's not hard to do!

Chapter Eleven

Set Up a Budget

WHEN I WAS A teenager, my parents seemed to be able to do or buy anything they wanted. We were far from rich, but my brother and I never wanted for anything. By the time I was married and the kids started coming along, my parents were traveling quite a bit. My husband and I looked up to them and thought we could live like that, too. We worked hard just like my parents, so we figured we could afford the same luxuries they were enjoying.

It wasn't until many years later, after many credit card balances had grown and grown, that we realized what we had done. Once we were faced with unemployment and mounting debt, we were finally forced to sit down and write out a budget. At that point we had no choice. We needed to see where our money was going so we could figure out where to cut expenses.

What a shock. After writing down every penny that left our household, we learned that we were spending a lot more than we were bringing in even before my husband became unemployed. The consequences of all those years of living like my parents and other financially stable couples came crashing down on us. Talk about a reality check!

When we were living like my parents, we weren't thinking about how long it had taken them to become financially stable enough to afford luxuries and traveling. I love the saying "My overnight success took me twenty-five years" because it rings true in so many ways. The truth is that very few people become successful overnight. It may look like that, but what we don't see are the years and years of dedication and hard work that led to their success. The same was true when I looked at my parents. The years that my mother drove around in a car that was on its last legs was a distant memory to me. By the time I was an adult and had a family of my own, I'd long forgotten about the old Chevelle she'd driven for so many years before they were able to afford a nice car. The Chevelle had a hole in the floor, and when it rained the carpet would get wet. After a while, tiny seedlings would start to sprout in the carpet—really. And when we turned the heat on, it sounded like a train was coming down the street. Yikes!

I'd also forgotten that my dad did all the construction and repair on our house and that there were many years when we didn't go on vacation. Those were also the years my mom sometimes got up at three a.m. to beat a snowstorm and get to work on time. But I didn't remember any of that. What stuck in my mind was how I saw them living many years later. Twenty-five years later, to be exact. Their financial success took them two and half decades, and I wanted to be in the same place as them in just one year.

Unfortunately, it took us twenty-five years and a lot of financial damage to realize we were going about it all wrong. Had we started our married life with a budget, we would have known from day one where our money was going and what our limits actually were. So there we were, twenty-five years into our marriage, finally making a budget, shredding our credit cards, and starting from scratch. Well, actually we started from below scratch, but we started.

Preparing a budget is the most important thing we've ever done. It has helped us to become more focused on our spending, pay off our debt, reevaluate our wants and needs, and, truth be told, live a much simpler, happier life. Budgets allow you to know where your money is going rather than wondering where it went. Who would have thought that a budget could do all that? It can!

I believe so wholeheartedly in preparing a budget and following one that I talk about it with any young adult willing to listen. I preach it to my kids all the time, and now my daughters both follow very strict budgets of their own. I'm still working on my son, who recently graduated from college, but I'm hoping it will click for him one day.

I highly suggest a zero-based budget. This is a budget that accounts for every single penny that comes in and every single penny that goes out. At the end of the budget period, which could be a week, two weeks, a month, or a year, if you have any money left, immediately put it into a savings budget account. Your goal is to grow that savings budget over time. Be sure to set up a bank account for yourself that's strictly for savings. If you set up realistic budget categories for yourself, you'll set aside all the money you need for your expenses, including the unexpected.

Here are some steps you can take to get your budget in tip-top shape and keep all that money you're saving on groceries instead of spending it on unnecessary items:

1. Go through your income and expenses. Look at every single bit of income that comes in and every single bit that goes out. Write it all down. Everything. Every gift, every fast-food purchase, everything. Once you have it all written down,

start with the items that are due every month and can't be changed (at least not right away). These are called "fixed bills." Fixed bills include mortgage or rent, car payments, phone bills, and tuition. Then make a list of the bills you *can* adjust. These are called "variable bills." Variable bills include bills for groceries, gas, dining out, entertainment, clothing, and gifts.

2. Write your budget. If your mortgage or rent is $2,000 a month and you're budgeting every two weeks, $1,000 per biweekly paycheck gets put aside for that. If you get paid weekly, you would be setting aside $500 a week toward your mortgage or rent. If you get a monthly paycheck, the full $2,000 would be set aside each time you're paid. Go down the list and account for everything. If you don't make enough to cover everything you listed, you'll need to make adjustments. This is a must. Your outgoing cash *must not* exceed your incoming cash. If it does, go to your variable bills and start cutting. If you have money left over, it should be used to pay down debt or add to your emergency fund, savings account, and/or retirement account.

3. If you don't have an emergency fund, you need to add that to your budget. Get yourself to save $1,000 as quickly as possible. If it means selling off some stuff on eBay or at a garage sale, do it. If it means eating out of your stockpile for a month or two, do it. It's very important to have a small emergency fund so that when something goes wrong, you don't have to pull out a credit card to pay for it.

4. Designate money from each paycheck for cash envelopes. This is money that you would usually spend during your regular errands. Once you run out of the money in these envelopes, you'll need to wait until you get your next paycheck to add to it. This really forces you to control your spending.

Here are some categories we use for our cash envelopes:

- Groceries
- Gas
- Clothes
- Haircuts
- Pet supplies/food
- Dry cleaning
- Extra spending money for my husband

- Extra spending money for myself

Extra spending money is just that—money we can put in our wallets and spend on whatever extra things we want. Twenty-five dollars isn't much to get us through two weeks, but it's nice to have some extra cash in our wallets.

5. When we first started on our budget, my biggest problem wasn't with the money that we pulled out for the cash envelopes, but with the money that was budgeted and left in our bank account. I didn't want it to just sit in one account in one lump. I wanted it to be in envelopes like our cash envelopes so that it was set aside for the budget item it was intended for. So the money in the bank was a larger challenge to organize.

We use Quicken to manage our checking and savings accounts, so to solve this problem I decided to track our bank money by setting up separate Quicken accounts—"envelopes"—within my larger account. Each new account was named for its respective budget item, such as "Mortgage" or "Phone bill." My money still stays in one account at my bank—I just show it in Quicken as moving from the main account to its budget account. When I go to pay my mortgage, buy a present, or have the car repaired, the money has already been accounted for in the individual account, or "virtual envelope."

Though I do this in Quicken, you could do it in Excel or even use the free software Mint to manage your budget. Some bank accounts now offer this online as well. Even old-fashioned pen and paper will work. Whatever works for you and your family.

Here are some of the virtual envelopes you should set up. Ultimately, they should be personalized for you and your family, so your list will look a little different from this one:

- Mortgage or rent
- Phone
- Internet
- Car payment
- Car repair
- House repair
- Hospitality
- Gifts
- Savings
- Car insurance

- Car replacement
- College tuition
- Utilities
- Emergency fund
- Health
- Memberships
- Life insurance
- Miscellaneous
- Vacation

Remember, this is in addition to the cash envelopes you set up in Step 4.

6. Once your budget is set, the key is to stick with it. It's easy to pull from one of your budgeted accounts one month to pay for another budget that has run dry. The typical thing to do is to say, "Hey, I'll pay it back next paycheck." Truth be told, nine times out of ten that won't happen. The money never gets back to where it should be, and before you know it, you've dug a little hole that you're having trouble climbing out of. What happens next? Those credit cards come out to pay for the stuff you had on your budget that you can no longer keep up with.

Setting up a budget and sticking to it are, in my opinion, the most important parts of the process of gaining control of your finances. It doesn't matter if you make $15,000 a year or $250,000 a year—everyone needs a budget they can stick to and follow. It's not easy in the beginning, but nothing that's worth your while is ever easy.

You will see, as time goes on, that following your budget becomes a way of life. Once you start looking at your finances that way, you'll never go back. It will be the most important thing you do, not just for your finances but also for your relationship, your health, and your peace of mind. Yep, a budget can do all that!

Chapter Twelve

Be in Control of Your Spending

S o how does a budget really help your marriage? And better yet, how does it help your health?

Consider my own story. Pat and I had been happily married for twenty-five years, or so we thought. We would spend and spend, buying anything we wanted. We built up quite a bit of debt over the years, which caused a lot of tension in our marriage. Occasionally, we had so much debt that we had to refinance our home or get a home-equity loan. Each time this happened, there were a lot of questions about how we'd let our financial situation get so bad, a lot of finger-pointing. There were times when we were worried about not being able to pay for the essentials. The stress made us snap over the smallest issues.

For months we would happily spend whatever we wanted but would then be faced with unexpected expenses we couldn't pay for. Like the times we had to spend $3,000 to repair our roof, $2,500 to repair our car, and $4,000 to get a new heating system for the house. With mounting debt and no extra income, tensions would run high as we tried to figure out where to get the money. Refinancing our mortgage or pulling out money from the equity in our home was the only way we could do it. This was a temporary fix to a problem that took us decades to recognize.

Fast-forward to 2009, when Pat was unemployed twice and the housing market had dropped, causing the value of our home to drop as well. That meant that the equity we could tap into was greatly reduced. Our go-to solution for dealing with unexpected financial burdens was gone. Seriously stressed out, we argued often because we couldn't figure out how to pull ourselves out of this situation. We did and still do have a happy marriage, but it used to be filled with all this unnecessary tension.

As you know by now, couponing and setting up a strict budget were our lifesavers. The first six months were hard because we eliminated almost everything we possibly could from our lifestyle. We didn't eat out, buy clothes, or buy anything that wasn't absolutely necessary. We even sold some possessions to build up our emergency fund. It was rough, but together we decided that this was the change we needed after all those years of living without a budget.

After six months, Pat got another job. But at this point we were so focused on paying off our debt the right way rather than using the equity in our home that we continued to live under this strict budget for two and a half more years. It was hard, but we were happier than we'd been in years! We had a shared goal of paying off our debt. The budget we had set up allowed us the peace of mind of knowing that, although we still had debt, we had control of our money. There was no stress, no arguing. If we didn't have the money to do something, we didn't do it. We said no to a lot of things, and it was a long three years, but we did it. At the end of those three years, we'd paid off all our debt! It was the most rewarding feeling in the world.

At this point, we could have gone on a spending spree like we used to do, especially since we were both working and had a decent income. And with no debt, well, we had extra money each month. But instead, we loosened up our budget a bit by giving ourselves more breathing room. We increased our budget amounts for things like vacation, eating out, and clothes, but we continued to use coupons to save thousands on groceries. Staying on our budget allowed us to build our savings and prepare for the unexpected.

And good thing, because the unexpected happened. Not once but twice. The first time was in 2012, not long after we had paid off all our debt. Our son, Patrick, who was at college out of state, was attacked by a stranger with a golf club while walking down the street. He was rushed into trauma surgery with internal bleeding. Pat and I drove the twelve hours from New Jersey directly to the hospital and stayed in town until Patrick was discharged after a week. Our expenses, including travel, hotel, food, and medical bills, totaled more than $10,000. But we were prepared! And because we were prepared, we could focus on his recovery and not worry about how much we were spending.

The second unexpected event happened early in 2014. A division of Pat's company was shut down, and we were once again faced with unemployment. But the call he made to me while he was waiting his turn to be told (more than 150 employees were notified one by one) was so much different from the calls back in 2009. We were both calm and relaxed and joked that maybe at fifty-five years old, he should just retire. It was a completely different feeling. There was no panic, no blaming, no arguing. We knew our financial situation, and we knew that we could make this all work. We were ready!

So how can sticking to a budget help your marriage and your health? The stress of not having control of your finances is more than some people and some marriages can handle. Dealing with unexpected expenses when you're not prepared for them can be bad for your health and turn a happy marriage into one long "he said, she said" argument. Having complete control of your money does the complete opposite. It brings peace and calm to you and your family because you know you're ready to conquer the unexpected events that happen in all of our lives.

We're living proof that control of your finances can reduce the stress of your marriage and allow you to live a fuller, richer life.

Closing Note

U SING COUPONS HAS CHANGED my family forever.
What started out as a way to put food on our table
during difficult financial times evolved into a way
of life that's debt-free. It allows us to live rich without
overspending! If someone told me ten years ago that using
coupons could do all that for me, I probably would have
laughed. But it really is true. Going from being in debt
and jobless to having the financial freedom to not worry
about what may come next in life is truly empowering.
I'm happier, my husband's happier, and our entire family
has so much less stress and more fun. We live a simpler
life now and will continue to live this way for the rest of
our lives.

I want that same financial freedom for you. I've shed
tears reading e-mails from LivingRichWithCoupons.com

readers who have shared the stories of how couponing has transformed their lives. It keeps me motivated to continue teaching and guiding people to save on their groceries.

I wish you all the best on your couponing journey, and remember, successful couponers aren't born—we're made. Saving thousands of dollars won't happen overnight, but if you follow the guidance in this book, it *will* happen. Give yourself time and patience to make it work and you'll be well on your way to living rich with coupons!

Keep on couponing!

—Cindy

About the Author

CINDY LIVESEY IS ON a mission to help people save money and live richer lives! *The Rachael Ray Show*'s coupon expert, Cindy created her website, Living Rich With Coupons, in 2009 to share her couponing strategies and tips with family and friends. Within a year, the site had more traffic than it could handle, so she upgraded it and turned it into a full-service couponing mecca.

Cindy came up with her couponing strategies when her husband's job was eliminated and she was forced to put her household on a budget. By strategically using coupons, she saved $11,000 on groceries in one year! Through Living Rich With Coupons, Cindy and her team provide thousands of people with a money-saving approach that will allow them to pay off debt, save for vacations, pay college tuition, buy new cars, and even splurge on a designer handbag.

Resources

Couponing Lingo

Blinkie: Nickname for the Smart Source machines found in most stores. They are those little red boxes that hang from store shelves and dispense coupons.

B1G1/BOGO: Buy one, get one free.

BOGO 50%: Buy one, get one at 50 percent off.

CAT: Catalina coupons that the cashier prints in the store. The machines are provided and operated by a company called Catalina Marketing.

DND: Do not double.

ECB: ExtraCare Bucks from CVS.

eCoupon: Coupons, usually store coupons, that are loaded directly to your store loyalty cards.

Hang tags: Coupons found hanging on products.

IP: Internet-printed coupon.

ISO: In search of…

MIR: Mail-in rebate.

Mfg: Manufacturer coupon.

MM: Moneymaker.

NLA: No longer available.

OOP: Out of pocket.

OYNO: On your next order.

P&G: Procter & Gamble insert.

Peelies: Coupons attached to products.

psa: Prices start at.

Price-matching: Using a competitor's price to reduce the price you pay at another store.

PP: Price plus from Shoprite.

Rain check: Store-issued credit that allows you to purchase products at the sale price at a later date.

Rebate: A refund of part or all of the amount you paid for an item, obtained by submitting the receipt to the manufacturer.

RP: RedPlum insert.

RR: Register Rewards (Walgreens).

SCR: Single check rebate (Rite Aid).

SS: SmartSource insert.

Stacking: Using store coupons in tandem with manufacturer coupons.

Stockpile, noun: A large supply of food gathered and held in reserve for use during a shortage or during a period of higher prices.

Stockpile, verb: To accumulate for future use; put or store in a stockpile.

Tear Pads: Coupon pads located in stores to promote products.

UPC: Universal product code.

Wags: Walgreens.

YMMV: Your miles may vary (when talking about your particular store as compared with another store).

WYB: When you buy.

$1/2: $1 off of two items.

Internet Coupons

- Checkout51.com
- CommonKindness.com
- Coupons.com
- Hopster.com
- Ibotta.com
- MamboSprouts.com
- SavingStar.com
- SmartSource.com
- RedPlum.com
- coupons.target.com/
- cartwheel.target.com

(Applications)

- Checkout 51
- BerryCart
- Ibotta
- Snap By Groupon

Magazines With Coupons Included:

- *All You*
- *Better Homes & Gardens*
- *Shape*
- *Woman's Day*

For Consumer Information

(Clean Fifteen & Dirty Dozen, etc.)

- EWG.org

For Healthy Recipes

- www.mywholefoodlife.com

For Healthy Food Sources

- www.localharvest.org/food-coops/
- www.localharvest.org/csa/

For Freezing and Canning Information

- *Preserving Summer's Bounty: A Quick and Easy Guide to Freezing, Canning, Preserving, and Drying What You Grow*, by the Rodale Food Center and Susan McClure.

For Tips on Budgeting

- www.daveramsey.com/get-started/

For Managing Your Budget

- Quicken
- Excel
- Mint (free software)

Store Coupon Policies

CVS

CVS/PHARMACY COUPONS (EXTRABUCKS® REWARDS and ExtraCare® Coupons) and third-party manufacturer coupons are accepted in our retail stores in accordance with the following guidelines:

- CVS/pharmacy does not accept expired coupons.
- CVS/pharmacy will not accept third-party manufacturers' coupons with another retailer's logo.
- Coupons cannot be exchanged for cash or gift cards.
- Third-party manufacturer coupons are issued by a third party, and sales tax may be charged on pre-coupon price.
- CVS/pharmacy does not accept coupons for items not carried in our stores.

- CVS/pharmacy accepts only ExtraBucks Rewards applicable to the ExtraCare card offered at time of purchase.
- CVS/pharmacy does not accept coupon bar-code images displayed on a smartphone, iPhone, Droid, etc.
- The total value of the coupons may not exceed the value of the transaction. Sales tax must be paid if required by state law.
- Certain CVS/pharmacy coupons may be subject to state sales-tax rules similar to third-party manufacturer coupons, and sales tax may be charged on pre-coupon price
- Language at the bottom of CVS/pharmacy coupons provides specific coupon acceptance rules.
- Any coupon offer not covered in these guidelines may be accepted at the discretion of CVS management.

Sale Items

- CVS/pharmacy will accept manufacturer coupons for an item that is on sale.
- CVS/pharmacy will not accept percent-off coupons for an item that is on sale.
- In the event that any item's price is less than the value of the coupon, CVS/pharmacy will accept the coupon only to the price of the item.

- CVS/pharmacy does not provide cash back in exchange for any coupons.

Multiple Coupons

- CVS/pharmacy accepts one manufacturer coupon and applicable CVS/pharmacy coupon(s) per item unless prohibited by either coupon offer.
- There is no limit to the number of ExtraBucks Rewards that may be used in a transaction as long as it does not exceed the transaction total.
- The number of manufacturer coupons used in a transaction may not exceed the number of items in the transaction.
- The coupon amount will be reduced if it exceeds the value of the item after other discounts or coupons are applied. (For example, a $5 coupon for a $4.99 item will result in a $4.99 coupon value).
- CVS/pharmacy accepts multiple identical coupons for multiple qualifying items as long as there is sufficient stock to satisfy other customers, unless a limit is specified. Management reserves the right to limit the quantity of items purchased.
- CVS/pharmacy reserves the right to process coupons in any order.

- CVS/pharmacy accepts multiple dollar-off-transaction coupons (e.g., $3 off $15) in one transaction if they apply.
    - Ex. Customers may use two $3-off-$15 coupons if they are purchasing over $30.

Buy One, Get One Free Coupons

- Sales tax must be paid for any Buy One, Get One Free coupon offer if required by applicable state laws.
- Two coupons may be used on a Buy One, Get One Free promotion as long as their total does not exceed the item total.
    - Ex. Suave Shampoo is on sale for $2, buy one, get one free, and the customer is purchasing two shampoos; customer may use two coupons for $1 each and pay the applicable tax.
- Buy One, Get One Free promotions may be combined with Buy One, Get One Free coupons. Customers are responsible for paying applicable tax.
    - Ex. Suave Shampoo is on sale for $2, BOGO, and customer has an MFG coupon for Suave BOGO. Customer will receive both items for free but will need to pay any applicable tax.

Internet/Print-at-Home Coupons

- CVS/pharmacy accepts Internet/print-at-home coupons that include a bar code.
- CVS/pharmacy will not accept reproductions or rebates.

Dollar General

DOLLAR GENERAL IS PLEASED to accept manufacturers' coupons and Dollar General Store coupons at any of our more than 10,000 stores. These coupons come from a variety of sources, including, but not limited to, newspapers, magazines, print-at-home (Internet), direct mail, product packaging, and in-store coupon boxes.

Our coupon requirements are as follows:

> Dollar General accepts manufacturers' and Dollar General-issued coupons (including Internet coupons) that meet these requirements:

1. Coupons must be original (no photocopies).

2. Coupons must have a scannable bar code or valid promotion code.

3. Coupons must have a printed expiration date.

4. Coupons can be redeemed only for items sold at Dollar General, and can be redeemed only for the exact same item (package weight, size, etc.).

5. Coupons for free items are accepted only if a purchase is required to get one free.

6. Maximum of two coupons per item. One coupon must be a manufacturers' coupon, and the second coupon must be a Dollar General coupon as long as neither coupon states that it is not valid with other coupons.

Dollar General will *NOT accept coupons that:*

1. Are from other retailers

2. Are expired

3. Are Internet coupons without a scannable bar code and/or promotion code

4. Contain the combination of an invalid bar code that won't scan and a promotion code that the register will not accept

5. Are for "free" items unless a purchase is required (i.e., Buy One, Get One Free is acceptable)

6. Do not have a "remit to" address on the coupon

   In addition: "Cash back" will not be issued if the value of the coupon is greater than the purchase price of the item.

Dollar Tree

Manufacturer Coupons

- We accept manufacturer coupons only. We do not accept retail-specific coupons, such as those of Target, Walmart, etc.
- We do not accept photocopies of coupons. Coupons must be intact and not altered or modified in any way.
- Coupons can be used only in stores, must be presented at time of purchase, and cannot be redeemed for cash at a later time.
- Item purchased must match the coupon description (brand, size, quantity, color, etc.) and be presented prior to the expiration date printed on the coupon.

- We accept only one manufacturer coupon per single item purchased.
- We accept coupons for over a dollar on a single item, but the coupon value will be reduced to the purchase price of the item.
- We cannot give cash back if the face value of a coupon is greater than the purchase price of the item.
- We accept coupons for over a dollar on multiple items if the coupon amount does not exceed the combined retail price of the items indicated.
- We accept up to four like coupons per household per day.
- Coupons for free items are accepted only if a purchase is required to get one free (for example, Buy One, Get One Free offers).
- Any applicable sales tax must be paid by consumer.
- We reserve the right to accept, refuse or limit the use of any coupon.
- This policy is subject to all local, state, and federal laws and regulations where applicable.
- These guidelines apply to all coupons accepted at Dollar Tree (manufacturer and Internet coupons).

Internet Coupons

- We accept up to two Internet coupons per household per day.
- Internet coupons must be manufacturers' coupons, have valid expiration dates, and have valid remit addresses for the manufacturers.
- We do not accept Internet coupons for "free" items with no purchase requirements.
- Duplicated (photocopied) Internet coupons will not be accepted. Each Internet coupon must have a different serial number.

Family Dollar

FAMILY DOLLAR STORES ACCEPT manufacturer and Family Dollar-issued coupons, including:

- Printed coupons
- Internet coupons
- Mobile coupons

Family Dollar Stores ACCEPTS manufacturer and Family Dollar-issued coupons that meet these requirements:

- Only one manufacturer coupon and one Family Dollar coupon can be used per item in a transaction.

- Duplicate coupons in one transaction are accepted as long as there is an item purchased for each coupon.
- All Family Dollar coupons must have a scannable bar code or valid promotion code.
- Printed coupons must be original (no photocopies) and have a printed expiration date.
- Internet coupons may be in either black-and-white or color and must be legible and read "Family Dollar" or "manufacturer coupon."
- Mobile coupons must have a valid promotion code.

Please note:
- Coupons can be redeemed only for items that are described on the coupon. The copy on the coupon dictates which items are to be included in the offer, not the image of what is shown on the coupon.
- Coupons can be redeemed if the value of the coupon is greater than the price of the item. In this case, the value of the coupon will be discounted to match the price of the item.
- Buy One, Get One Free coupons are accepted only if the exact same two products are the "buy" and the "free."

- Family Dollar $5-off-$25 coupon is accepted as long as the net purchase, after all other offers, coupons, and/or discounts have been applied, is $25 or more.
- Coupons are acceptable for use on sale or clearance items.

Family Dollar does not accept coupons that:
- Are from other retailers
- Are expired
- Are for "free" items that do not require a purchase. We do accept coupons for items that are equal to or greater than the price of the item and reduce the price to free.
- Are manufacturer coupons that do not have a "remit to" address on the coupon
- Are bottle caps

Please note:
- Competitor coupons are not matched.

Kroger

Kroger Print-at-Home Coupon Acceptance Policy

EFFECTIVE NOVEMBER 2007, ALL Kroger divisions accept industry-standard, secure print-at-home coupons. We recently partnered with Coupons Inc., the industry leader in print-at-home coupons, to offer print-at-home coupons on Kroger.com and all of our store banner websites. You may also find coupons on brand websites and legitimate coupon websites like Coupons.com. Help us make your shopping experience a pleasant one by keeping in mind these simple rules for using print-at-home coupons.

We can accept print-at-home coupons only if they scan properly at checkout. Legitimate printable coupons are delivered using special software designed to print a properly rendered bar code on the coupon and limit the number of coupons printed.

We will generally not accept "free product" (no purchase required) print-at-home coupons. It is currently an industry practice not to produce print-at-home manufacturer's coupons for free product. Buy One, Get One Free coupons and other values that have a purchase requirement are acceptable.

We will usually not accept coupons for more than about 75 percent of a product's value. For example, a $2-off coupon will be acceptable for a product that normally sells for $5 or more, but a $2-off printable coupon for a product that sells for $2.25 is unlikely to be legitimate. If there are exceptions, we are usually provided advance notice by the manufacturer.

Coupons will be rejected if they appear to be distorted or blurry, altered in any way, or are obvious duplicates. You should always print the coupon yourself directly from the website or e-mail that is offering it. Only then can you ensure you are printing a legitimate coupon. The coupon will never appear on your computer screen. A legitimate coupon is never sent as a graphic or PDF or sent in a Word document.

Print-at-home coupons should never be copied, sold, or traded. They should not be photocopied or scanned and distributed to others. They have unique serial numbers printed on them and follow an industry-standard format. Coupons are never sold, and you should not pay for someone's "time to clip" or other service fee.

Digital Coupons Policy

CUSTOMERS CHOOSING TO PARTICIPATE in the digital coupons are required to have an active online account with a valid associate shopper card. Kroger employees or partners are prohibited from setting up or otherwise maintaining an online account not specifically associated with that employee or employee household.

A valid shopper card or an alternate ID is required for the use of digital coupons at the time of purchase.

Digital coupons and offers are deducted from a customer purchase prior to paper coupons or any other discounts and cannot be added back or removed once card has been scanned.

- Limit one use per digital coupon per transaction.
- Digital offers cannot be combined with manufacturer paper coupons on the purchase of a single item.
- Digital offers do not double.
- A limit of 150 coupons can be loaded per household at one time.
- Digital reproductions of offers will not be accepted (such as using a mobile application to reproduce an image of an offer/coupon).

The store manager has the right to accept, decline or limit the use of any digital coupon or offer.

Publix

Publix Coupon Policy Q&A

PUBLIX ACCEPTS MANUFACTURERS' COUPONS (limit one per item), Publix coupons, valid Internet coupons, and coupons from nearby competitors identified for each Publix store. (Competitor names are posted at each Publix store.) All coupons must be originals—no copies.

- We will accept coupons from competing pharmacies for prescriptions only.
- We will not accept percent-off-items or percent-off-total-order coupons.
- We will accept coupons only for identical merchandise we sell.
- Acceptance is subject to any restrictions on the coupon, and we reserve the right to limit quantities.
- Manager approval is needed for individual coupons above $5.
- For a Buy One, Get One Free offer, each item is considered a separate purchase.
- We will not accept coupons presented via a mobile phone or device.

- We will accept a manufacturer's coupon and either a Publix or a competitor coupon on the same item.
- Digital offers cannot be combined with manufacturer paper coupons on the purchase of a single item.
- Dollars-off-total-order coupons will be limited to one Publix and one competitor coupon per order.
- The order total must be equal to or greater than the combined purchase requirements indicated on the coupon(s) presented.

Buy One, Get One Coupons

Q: I have a Buy One, Get Two Free coupon from a competitor of Publix's. Will Publix accept it?

A: Yes. If you're purchasing the identical merchandise at Publix, we'll accept BOGO and Buy One, Get Two Free coupons from competitors' stores

Dollars-Off-Total-Order Coupons

Q: A competitor on a store's approved list is offering a $5-off-a-$25-order coupon when I sign up to receive communications from them. Will Publix take this coupon?

A: Yes. You've already signed up with the competitor to receive the coupon, so now all you have to do is purchase $25 worth of groceries.

Q: Will Publix accept a competitor's coupon that indicates I must present my retailer-rewards card to use the coupon?

A: Yes. Publix doesn't require that you use a reward card, but we would be happy to honor this coupon if you meet the other purchase requirements on the coupon.

Coupon Stacking

Q: Can a store coupon, competitor coupon, and manufacturer's coupon all be used for one item?

A: No. A manufacturer's coupon can be combined with a Publix coupon or a competitor's coupon, but not both.

Q: If an item already has a manufacturer's coupon attached, will Publix take an additional manufacturer's coupon on the item?

A: Sorry, but no. Publix will take an additional Publix or competitor's coupon, but we can take only one manufacturer's coupon for an item, regardless of where the coupon came from.

Q: I have a "$1 off the purchase of two items" manufacturer's coupon. Can another manufacturer's coupon be used for either of these items?

A: No. When the manufacturer issues a "$1 off the purchase of two items" coupon, it requires the purchase of two items. So, because you have to purchase both items to meet the coupon's requirements, a manufacturer's coupon has already been applied to both items.

Q: I have a BOGO manufacturer's coupon. Can another manufacturer's coupon be used for either of these items?

A: No. When the manufacturer issues a BOGO coupon, it requires the purchase of two items. So, because you have to purchase both items to meet the coupon's requirements, a manufacturer's coupon has already been applied to both items.

Gift Card Coupons

Q: Will Publix accept a competitor's coupon for a free $5 gift card with the purchase of an item or items (e.g., a coupon for "Buy both Raid Max Bug Barriers 1 gallon Starter Kit and Refill, Receive a $5 store gift card").

A: Yes, if we carry the identical items named on the coupon, you'll receive a $5 Publix gift card with the required purchase.

Pharmacy Coupons

Q: Does Publix accept prescription coupons from all pharmacies or only from your listed competitors?

A: Publix accepts coupons for prescriptions from all local retail pharmacies.

Rain Checks and Coupons

Q: What if I have a rain check and a coupon for an item but the coupon is expired, though it was valid on the date the rain check was issued. Can I still use the coupon on the item?

A: Yes, Publix will accept the coupon that was valid on the date the rain check was issued.

Private-Label Coupons

Q: Will Publix accept a competitor's coupon for a private-label item?

A: Yes. We're happy to accept a coupon for a competitor's private-label product because it's a chance to introduce you to our terrific Publix brand.

Rite Aid

AT RITE AID, WE gladly accept many coupon types— including manufacturer coupons found in newspapers and magazines, as well as print-at-home coupons—to ensure you get the most value for your dollar. We accept the following coupon types as detailed in the coupon acceptance guidelines listed below:

Manufacturer Coupons

Manufacturer coupons are found in newspapers, magazines, and even affixed to products. The UPC on these coupons begins with a "5."

Rite Aid Manufacturer Coupons

Rite Aid Manufacturer coupons generally appear in our weekly circular, on our website, and are sent to customers via email. These coupons are labeled "manufacturer coupon" and have a UPC that begins with "49."

Rite Aid Valuable Coupons

Rite Aid coupons are labeled "Valuable Coupon" and have a UPC that begins with "48."

Internet/Print-at-Home coupons

Rite Aid will accept internet/print at home coupons.

eCoupons

Rite Aid and its business partners make electronic coupons available that can be loaded directly on a wellness+ card or Plenti card. The register automatically "rings" the coupon when the qualifying item is scanned. eCoupons are subject to the same rules as other coupons as defined in

Buy One, Get One Free

Rite Aid accepts Buy One, Get One Free coupons, however only one coupon can be used for each pair of items purchased. A customer can use one "cents off" coupon (a coupon of fixed value such as $.50, $1.25, etc.) in conjunction with the item they are purchasing on a Buy One, Get One Free promotion (or with a Buy One, Get One Free coupon), although the value of the cents off coupon cannot exceed the selling price of the item. Customers can use up to two coupons with a Buy One, Get One at a percent off promotion, provided the total value of the coupons does not exceed the selling price of the two items combined.

Buy One, Get One Free coupons cannot be used in conjunction with a Buy One, Get One Free or with a Buy One, Get One at a percent off promotion.

Total Purchase Coupons

Rite Aid may feature total purchase coupons, which discount the total purchase amount based upon meeting specific requirements. For example, $5 off a $25 purchase price threshold coupon.

These coupons are accepted under the following conditions:

- The coupon is valid and in date; only one total purchase coupon per transaction.
- Total purchase equals or exceeds $25 before tax (before any coupons are applied).
- Coupons for individual items can also be used including another "48" coupon that is tied to an item in the transaction.
- Provided the total of items purchased is equal to or greater than the purchase requirement, other coupons can be used in conjunction with the total purchase coupon.

General Acceptance Guidelines

- Coupons must be valid and in date; coupons cannot be exchanged for cash.
- Register will validate coupon through scanning or keyed entry of the coupon UPC number.
- In the event that any item's selling price is less than the value of the coupon, Rite Aid will accept the coupon in exchange for the selling price of the item. Coupon redemption can never exceed the selling price of an item and no cash back is allowed.
- When making a return for a product that had a coupon attached, Rite Aid cannot refund cash for the value of the coupon and cannot return the coupon that was used.
- Rite Aid reserves the right to not accept any coupon where the validity or the coupon cannot be established.

Multiple Coupons

More than one coupon can be used on the purchase of a single item under the following conditions:

- All coupons match the item being purchased.
- The total of the coupons is equal to or less than the selling price of the item before sales tax

No more than one "48" Rite Aid Valuable coupon, one "49" Rite Aid Manufacturer coupon, and one "5" Manufacturer coupon can be used on a single item. Rite Aid may accept up to four identical coupons for the same number of qualifying items as long as there is sufficient stock to satisfy other customers within the store manager's sole discretion.

Safeway

Manufacturer and Store Coupons

1. We will redeem coupons only for the specific items included in our customer's purchase transaction. The redemption value will be as stated on the coupon, unless that value yields a final price for such item less than zero; if application of the redemption value yields a price less than zero, the coupon will be redeemed only for the amount that yields a zero price (our customer cannot net a cash credit or payout from a coupon purchase).

2. Paper coupons must be presented at the time of the purchase transaction. We will accept only coupons issued by Safeway or the manufacturer

of the relevant product. We will not accept photocopies of coupons.

3. Coupons are subject to advertised offer limitations and all other limitations and restrictions on the applicable coupon or product.

4. Coupons may not be applied against any free item received in any offer.

5. Coupons have no cash value.

6. Safeway will not accept manufacturer coupons (including, but not limited to, coupons issued through a Catalina or other in-store coupon dispenser) that display another retailer's logo or name unless such coupon is for a specific item with the same product identifiers as the product included in our customer's purchase transaction and is sold and available at the store.

7. We will not accept coupons unless they have an expiration date. Expired coupons will not be accepted.

8. We will not accept coupons that, in the determination of Safeway personnel, appear distorted or blurry or are altered in any way.

9. Sales taxes will be applied in accordance with the law of the applicable state, regardless of any coupon or other discount that may apply to the purchase transaction.

10. All applicable bottle and packaging deposits on the purchased and free items must be paid by the customer.

11. Safeway reserves the right to refuse any coupons at its discretion.

12. Purchase-reward thresholds (if any) will be calculated based upon customer's final price (after deducting Club Card savings and all other discounts and savings) before deductions for any manufacturer coupons. As an example (and not as an offer), if a $10 minimum purchase is required for a customer reward, a customer's order at full retail would be $12, a Club Card discount of $1.75 applies, and a manufacturer's coupon of $1 applies, the customer would be given credit

for a $10.25 purchase and would be eligible for the reward (assuming compliance with all other requirements) even though the customer's cash payment would be only $9.25. The manufacturer's coupon would not be deducted from the total for purposes of determining reward eligibility. Purchase-reward thresholds (if any) will be calculated based upon customer's final price (after deducting Club Card savings and all other discounts).

13. References to a threshold purchase requirement will exclude purchases of beer, wine, spirits, tobacco products, fuel, all fluid items in the refrigerated dairy section (including fluid dairy and dairy substitutes), prescription items and co-payments, bus/commuter passes, fishing/hunting licenses and tags, postage stamps, money orders, money transfers, ski tickets, amusement-park tickets, event tickets, lottery tickets, phone cards, gift cards, and gift certificates. Also excluded are bottle deposits, redemption values, and sales taxes.

Internet-Printed Coupons

14. We accept Internet-printed coupons. The same manufacturer and store coupon rules above apply to all Internet-printed coupons.

15. Internet-printed coupons must be capable of scanning at checkout.

16. Internet-printed coupons must have serial numbers and must follow an industry-standard format.

17. Manufacturer Internet-printed coupons must clearly indicate that they are a manufacturer coupon and must have a valid manufacture address on the printed coupon.

18. We will not accept "free product" Internet-printed manufacturer coupons.

Load-to-Card Club Coupons

19. Internet and digital coupons that have been electronically loaded to a Safeway Club Card are automatically redeemed at the time of purchase after the Club Card number has been entered. All other coupon policies above apply to electronic

coupons that are loaded to a Club Card. Internet and digital coupons electronically loaded to a Safeway Club Card are not included in any operative "double coupon" or other increase in coupon value promotion. Coupons are not accepted on online shopping orders made on Safeway.com, except Internet and digital coupons that have been electronically loaded to the Safeway Club Card being used for that order.

Doubling of Coupons

20. Check with your local store regarding "double coupon" promotions where customers will receive double the manufacturer coupon face value off the regular or Club Card price up to the identified limit. Not all locations offer double coupon promotions, and the terms of such promotions may differ by time and store. Limitations and restrictions for double coupon promotions may change at any time. Changes will be posted in store only. "Double coupon" promotions do not apply to any Internet or digital coupons except for applicable Internet-printed manufacturer coupons. These explanations and restrictions on

"double coupons" apply to any promotion that increases the value of a manufacturer coupon beyond its face value.

Coupon Stacking

21. Safeway does not allow a customer to redeem two or more manufacturer coupons against the same item in a single transaction.

22. Coupon stacking policies for manufacturer coupons apply to paper and electronic coupons that have been loaded to a Club Card.

23. If a customer presents two coupons for the same item in a single transaction, Safeway will give the highest discount for that item, subject to the terms of the applicable offer and/or coupon.

Rain checks

24. Rain checks are for one-time use only.

25. Rain checks expire ninety days from the date issued and will be accepted at any Safeway store that has the specific item in stock.

26. We reserve the right to limit rain check quantities based on product availability and advertised limits.

27. Rain checks can be issued for up to six items unless otherwise stated in the applicable advertisement.

28. Rain checks will not be issued for beer, wine, spirits, tobacco products, fuel, all fluid items in the refrigerated dairy section (including fluid dairy and dairy substitutes).

29. Rain checks can be offered for store super coupon items unless otherwise specified on the coupon. Rain checks will not be provided for items advertised as "clearance," "while supplies last," "limited quantities," or other designation indicating a limited supply.

   All coupon redemption terms are subject to our Coupon Acceptance Policy in effect at time of redemption.

   We may change the terms of our Coupon Acceptance Policy at any time. Such changes may become effective without advance notice or advertisement. The current Coupon Acceptance

Policy will be posted at the customer service area in each store. You are also advised to periodically check our website for any changes to the terms of our Coupon Acceptance Policy.

Shoprite

<u>Wakefern Food Corp. Coupon Policy for Shoprite® Stores</u>

AT SHOPRITE®, WE KNOW that coupons are an important tool to help you save money. That's why it's our goal to make using coupons at Shoprite® stores easy for our customers. We welcome all Shoprite®-issued coupons along with valid manufacturer-issued coupons, valid Internet coupons, and valid electronic coupons loaded on your Price Plus® club card.

Shoprite® stores redeem coupons in accordance with manufacturer guidelines and the terms printed on the coupons. To help ensure product availability and an efficient checkout experience for all customers, the use of excessive amounts of coupons or multiple identical coupons may be limited at the store manager's discretion.

When redeeming coupons at Shoprite® stores, please be sure to:

1. Present your coupons at the time of purchase. Shoprite from Home® customers must present coupons when picking up an order or at the time of delivery. We cannot give cash back or credit for coupons not presented at time of purchase.

2. Present your Price Plus® club card to the cashier. Your card is required to redeem any digital coupons you may have loaded to your Price Plus® club card at shoprite.com. If you do not have your Price Plus® club card, you may access it by using the phone number on record in your Price Plus® club card profile. Customers who have downloaded the Shoprite mobile app may use the digital Price Plus® club card feature in the app. The Shoprite mobile app is the only app we will accept at the checkout in place of your Price Plus® club card.

3. Redeem your coupons within the time period printed on the coupon. We do not accept expired coupons.

4. Match your purchase to the specific item indicated on the coupon. No substitutions are permitted on manufacturer-issued coupons.

5. Use manufacturer-issued Internet coupons that are legible, with a valid remit address and a bar code that scans. Internet coupons that have been identified as counterfeit do not scan in our system and will not be accepted. We reserve the right to refuse any coupon for "free" product, Buy One, Get One Free offers, and those with a high value in relationship to the item's price.

6. Note your store's current double coupon policy. Double coupon policies vary by store. Check your store for details. We will double up to four identical coupons per household per day unless further restricted by the manufacturer.

Additional coupon restrictions are listed below:

7. We reserve the right to limit coupon redemptions to four of the same coupon per household per day.

8. Unless expressly prohibited by the terms on the coupon, we accept checkout (Catalina) coupons

and manufacturer-issued coupons that display other retailer logos only if they are clearly identified as manufacturer coupons and if they scan at checkout.

9. We do not accept coupons that have been identified as counterfeit and reserve the right to refuse any coupon that appears to be fraudulent. Coupons displaying signs of mass cutting or similar cuts and tears, coupons bearing tape, coupons in mint condition, and coupons bearing sequential numbers may suggest coupon fraud.

10. If the coupon's face value or multiplied value is greater than the purchase price of the item, we will give credit only up to the retail price of the item; we will not give cash back.

11. Only one manufacturer coupon will be applied to each Buy One, Get One Free offer.

12. We cannot refund the value of a coupon or return the coupon if a purchased item is later returned to the store.

13. Customers must pay any and all applicable taxes. The cash value of any Shoprite-issued coupon is 1/100¢.

14. Shoprite® stores do not accept coupons or savings offers presented in the form of a bar code on a mobile phone or other mobile electronic device.

15. Coupons are nontransferable and may not be copied, photocopied, scanned, altered, sold, traded or otherwise distributed to others. Coupons that are copied, photocopied, scanned, altered, sold, traded, distributed, or transferred by their original recipient to any other person, firm, or group are void.

Stop & Shop

Coupon Policy

TO ENSURE PRODUCT AVAILABILITY for all customers, we reserve the right to limit individual coupon quantities.

The value of the coupon will not be redeemed for more than the price of the item. Coupons have no cash value. Coupons must not be expired.

The physical coupon must be presented by the customer and retained by the cashier. Example: A coupon presented on a customer's personal device from an app (like Snip Snap) cannot be accepted.

Our stores do not accept altered or tampered (e.g.. expiration date cut off) or copied coupons.

Our stores do not accept competitor-issued store coupons. Exception: special circumstances that are communicated by the Division.

Unless a special store promotion is being run, we do not accept coupons for gift cards.

On manufacturers' coupons, sales tax will be applied to the total before the coupon is redeemed. The customer is responsible for the sales tax where required by law.

When using SNAP (food stamps) as payment, coupons will reduce the SNAP total due when redeemed toward the purchase of eligible food.

Manufacturer Coupon Policy

Our stores accept all manufacturer coupons. Exceptions are any items excluded by state regulations.

Only one manufacturer coupon may be used on each individual item purchased

The exact item stated on the coupon must be purchased in order to redeem the coupon.

Item substitutions are not allowed.

The maximum number of identical coupons allowed for each identical item is sixteen unless otherwise stated on the coupon.

Coupons may be redeemed on damaged or discontinued merchandise that has been reduced in price.

Any coupons for "free" products will be honored for the value of the item only. "Free" coupons cannot be doubled or tripled.

Store Coupon Policy

A paper store coupon, electronic store coupon, and manufacturer coupon may be redeemed on the same item. If the combined value for the coupons used exceeds the price of the item, the item is free. The manufacturer's coupon will be deducted first, and then the store coupon will be adjusted so that it does not exceed the price of the item.

Store coupons cannot be doubled or tripled.

Free Item and Buy One, Get One Free Manufacturer Coupon Policy

Free item manufacturer coupons may be used in conjunction with store instant BOGO offers. Example: first item scanned (manufacturer free coupon applied), second item scanned (store BOGO applied). Both items are free to the customer.

BOGO manufacturer coupon may be used in conjunction with store instant BOGO offers. Example: first item scanned (manufacturer BOGO applied), second item scanned (store BOGO applied). Both items are free to the customer.

To ensure product availability for all customers, we reserve the right to limit individual coupon redemption quantities.

Free Item and Two Like Manufacturer Coupon Policy

Two like manufacturer coupons may be used in conjunction with store instant BOGO offers. Example: first item scanned (manufacturer $1 coupon applied), second item scanned ($1 manufacturer coupon applied), store BOGO applied. Both items are eligible for $1 manufacturer coupon.

To ensure product availability for all customers, we reserve the right to limit individual coupon redemptions quantities.

Catalina Coupons

Our stores issue both manufacturer and store coupons from the Catalina printers at the time of checkout.

Our stores accept competitor-issued manufacturer Catalina coupons. Competitor issued Catalina coupons must specifically state "manufacturer coupon" to be accepted.

Catalina coupons cannot be doubled or tripled.

Item-specific manufacturer Catalina coupons cannot be used in conjunction with other manufacturer coupons for the same item.

Non-product-specific manufacturer Catalina coupons may be used in conjunction with manufacturer coupons. Example: $1-off-produce coupon.

Internet Coupons

We do accept Internet coupons, including those for a free item, with the following exceptions:

Coupon value cannot exceed $10.

If we are notified of fraudulent activity involving specific Internet coupons.

Internet coupons may be doubled provided they meet all doubling requirements and are not specifically prohibited by the manufacturer.

Double/Triple Coupon Policy:

Stores automatically double manufacturer coupons every day.

Coupons for lottery tickets, cigarettes, alcohol, and items prohibited by law are not to be doubled.

In order for a coupon to be doubled, the customer must use their loyalty card.

The Double Coupon Policy does not apply to "free" coupons, checkout coupons, eCoupons, Act Media coupons (where applicable), or store coupons.

We double the savings marked on any manufacturer's coupon up to $0.99. Any coupon $1 and greater will be redeemed at face value for the item purchased.

In cases where the double coupon total exceeds the value of the item, the offer is limited to the retail price.

The maximum number of identical coupons allowed for each identical item is sixteen unless otherwise stated on the coupon.

Internet coupons qualify to be doubled unless otherwise stated on the coupon. A maximum of four identical manufacturer's coupons may be doubled. Up to an additional 12 identical manufacturer's coupons can be redeemed at face value for a total of sixteen identical manufacturer's coupons. Example: If a customer purchased five boxes of Cheerios and presented five manufacturer's coupons for $0.50 each, the first four coupons would be doubled to $1. The fifth coupon would be redeemed for only $0.50.

Occasionally the company may participate in Dollar Doubler coupon promotions. When Dollar Doubler promotions are run, program details will be available in the circular.

Occasionally the company may participate in triple coupon promotions. When triple coupon promotions are run, program details will be available in the circular.

Internet coupons qualify to be doubled unless otherwise stated on the coupon.

eCoupons

Customers registered on our website can periodically load eCoupons to their loyalty cards from their accounts.

After eCoupons are loaded, the discount will automatically be applied at checkout if the qualifying product(s) are purchased using the same loyalty card the offers were loaded to.

eCoupons have an expiration date that is communicated on the website.

eCoupons will not double or triple.

eCoupons can be used in conjunction with manufacturer coupons and paper store coupons for the same item.

Target

Manufacturer and Target Coupons

- Target accepts one manufacturer coupon and one Target coupon for the same item (unless prohibited by either coupon).

- We reserve the right to accept, refuse or limit the use of any coupon.

- Limit of four identical coupons per household, per day (unless otherwise noted on coupon).

- All valid coupons should be presented to the cashier during checkout.

- Item purchased must match the coupon description (brand, size, quantity, color, flavor, etc.).

- Coupon amount may be reduced if it exceeds the value of the item after other discounts or coupons are applied.

- We can't give cash back if the face value of a coupon is greater than the purchase value of the item.

- All applicable sales taxes are paid by the guest at the full value of the item.

- These guidelines apply to all coupons accepted at Target (color checkout coupons, Internet coupons, mobile coupons, mailed coupons, coupons from newspapers and magazines, etc.).

Internet (Print-at-Home) Coupons

- We gladly accept valid Internet coupons that contain a clear and scannable bar code.
- We do not accept Internet coupons for free items with no purchase requirements.

Mobile Coupons

Guests can receive Target mobile coupons by signing up for text alerts at Target.com/mobile or by texting COUPONS to 827438 (TARGET). Message and data rates may apply. See site for full details. To redeem, simply show your coupon bar code to the cashier. With one simple scan, all applicable coupons are applied.

Buy One, Get One Free Coupons

- BOGO coupons cannot be combined (i.e., you cannot use two BOGO coupons on two items and get both for free). Unless stated otherwise on the coupon, the use of one Buy One, Get One Free coupon requires that two of the valid items are presented at checkout of which one item will be charged to the guest and the second item will be discounted by its full retail price.

- A second cents-off coupon of the same type cannot be redeemed toward the purchase price of the first item.
- If a Target BOGO coupon is used, one additional manufacturer coupon may be used on the first item.
- If a manufacturer BOGO coupon is used, one additional Target coupon may be used on the first item.

Returns

Returns of items purchased using manufacturer coupons may receive coupon value returned in the form of a Target gift card.

Exclusions

- Coupons are void if copied, scanned, transferred, purchased, sold, prohibited by law, or appear altered in any way.
- We regularly monitor the Coupon Information Corporation (CIC) website for counterfeit coupons. We do not accept counterfeit coupons.
- We can't accept coupons from other retailers or coupons for products not carried in our stores.
- Some items may not be available at all stores.
- We do not accept expired coupons.

- We do not accept Canadian coupons in our US stores.

Walgreens

Coupon Policy

As a customer-focused retailer, Walgreens encourages the use of coupons by our customers in our retail stores, in accordance with the following guidelines and as required by state and local laws. Note: This policy may change at any time without advance notice or advertisement. The coupon policy shall be made available upon request in store and online at Walgreens.com/CouponPolicy. Any coupon offer not covered in these guidelines shall be accepted at the discretion of Walgreens management.

General Guidelines

- All coupons are to be presented to the cashier at the time of checkout.
- Walgreens does not accept expired coupons. Coupons expire at 11:59 p.m. on the expiration date at the point of sale, whether in store or online.
- Walgreens will not accept fraudulent or counterfeit coupons as determined by Walgreens.
- Coupons and their face value cannot be exchanged for cash or gift cards.

- Competitors' coupons shall not be accepted by Walgreens.

- The number of manufacturer coupons, including Register Rewards®/Savings Rewards manufacturer coupons, shall not exceed the number of items in the transaction. The total value of the coupons shall not exceed the value of the transaction. Sales tax must be paid if required by state law.

- Walgreens will not accept coupons that exceed the selling price of an item, and no cash back is ever provided in exchange for any coupons.

- Coupons that appear to be distorted, blurry, or altered in any way shall not be accepted; all coupons must have a clear and scannable bar code.

- For offers when multiple items are purchased and additional items are free (buy one, get one free, etc.), the number of coupons applied to that offer cannot exceed the number of items required in the "buy" portion of the offer.

- Coupons may not be applied against any free item received in any offer (see above).

- Paper coupons will be processed before digital coupons.

- Walgreens shall not accept coupons for items not carried in our stores.

- Walgreens reserves the right to limit quantities to customers and employees.
- Manufacturer coupons must include a valid redemption address.
- Coupons may be subject to advertised offer limitations and all other limitations and restrictions on the applicable coupon or product.
- Walgreens shall accept manufacturer coupons for items that are on sale.
- The general guidelines apply to the categories below and are to be referenced in addition to the specific coupon category guidelines.

Multiple Coupons

When purchasing a single item, Walgreens accepts one manufacturer coupon and applicable Walgreens coupon(s) for the purchase of a single item, unless prohibited by either coupon offer.

When purchasing multiple items, Walgreens accepts multiple coupons for multiple qualifying items, as long as there is sufficient stock to satisfy other customers, unless a limit is specified on the coupon. Management reserves the right to limit the quantity of items purchased and/or prohibit the purchase of excessive quantities. An excessive quantity is any quantity above and beyond normal household usage.

Buy One, Get One Free Coupons

When items are featured in a Buy One, Get One Free promotion, at least one product needs to be purchased. A maximum of one BOGO coupon is permitted per two qualifying items in a BOGO offer.

Internet-printed Coupons

Walgreens shall not accept "free product" Internet-printed coupons.

Register Rewards®/Savings Rewards Coupons

- Register Rewards/Savings Rewards will print only for in-stock merchandise during the promotional period.
- Register Rewards/Savings Rewards can be earned only for eligible items. No substitutions are permitted.
- There is a limit of one Register Rewards/Savings Rewards coupon per offer per customer per transaction.
- Customers redeeming a Register Rewards/ Savings Rewards against the same offer may

not receive another Register Rewards/Savings Rewards coupon.

- Customers redeeming a Register Rewards/ Savings Rewards against the same offer may not receive another Register Rewards/Savings Rewards coupon.
- The number of manufacturer coupons, including Register Rewards/Savings Rewards manufacturer coupons, shall not exceed the number of items in the transaction.
- Register Rewards/Savings Rewards shall be forfeited if the qualifying merchandise is returned.
- Register Rewards/Savings Rewards can be redeemed for eligible items only. Ineligible items include but are not limited to:
  - Alcoholic beverages
  - Dairy products
  - Gift cards/phone cards/prepaid reloadable cards
  - Health care services, including immunizations
  - Lottery tickets
  - Money orders/transfers
  - Postage stamps
  - Prescription Savings Club membership fee
  - Prescriptions

- Special event/entertainment tickets or passes
- Tobacco products
- Transportation passes
- Any items prohibited by law

Digital/Paperless Coupons

Only digital coupons, attached to your Walgreens Balance® Rewards account, shall be honored. Digital reproductions of offers shall not be accepted (such as using a mobile application to reproduce an image of an offer/coupon).

Total Store Offer/Coupons

Total store offer/coupons cannot be combined—i.e., 20 percent off your whole purchase (circular coupon), Seniors Day, Friends and Family, Veterans Day, employee discount, etc.

Walmart

Print-at-Home Internet Coupons

- Must be legible
- Must have "Manufacturer Coupon" printed on them
- Must have a valid remit address for the manufacturer
- Must have a valid expiration date
- Must have a scannable bar code

- May not be duplicated
- Are acceptable in black and white or color

Manufacturers' Coupons

- Accepted for dollar/cents off
- Accepted for free items (except those printed off the Internet)
- Must have "Manufacturer Coupon" printed on them
- Must have a valid remit address for the manufacturer
- Must have a valid expiration date
- Must have a scannable bar code
- May not be duplicated

Competitors' Coupons

- Accepted for a specific item for a specified price
- Must have a valid expiration date
- Are acceptable in black and white

Soft Drink Container Caps

- Accepted

Checkout Coupons (Catalinas)

- May be printed at our competitors' registers for dollar/cents off on a specific item
- Must have "Manufacturer Coupon" with specific item requirements printed on them

- Must have a valid remit address for the manufacturer
- Must have a valid expiration date
- Must have a scannable bar code
- Are acceptable in black and white
- May not be duplicated

We do not accept the following coupons:

- Checkout coupons
    - Dollars/cents off the entire basket purchase
    - Percentage off the entire basket purchase
- Print-at-home Internet coupons that require no purchase
- Competitors' coupons
    - Dollars/cents off at a specific retailer
    - Percentage off
    - BOGO coupons without a specified price
    - Double- or triple-value coupons

Guidelines and Limitations

- We accept coupons only for merchandise that we sell.
- Coupons must be presented at the time of purchase.
- Only one coupon per item.
- Item purchased must be identical to the coupon (size, quantity, brand, flavor, color, etc.).

- There is no limit on the number of coupons per transaction.

- Coupons must have an expiration date and be redeemed prior to expiration.

- If coupon value exceeds the price of the item, the excess may be given to the customer as cash or applied toward the basket purchase.

- SNAP items purchased in a SNAP transaction are ineligible for cash back.

- WIC items purchased in a WIC transaction are applied to the basket purchase and may not be eligible for cash back. Refer to state-specific WIC guidelines.

- Great Value, Marketside, Equate, Parents Choice, and World Table coupons have no cash value and are ineligible for cash back or application to the basket purchase.

- The system will prompt for supervisor verification for:
  - Forty coupons per transaction
  - A coupon of $20 or greater on one item
  - $50 or more in coupons in one transaction

Acknowledgments

THIS BOOK HAS BEEN an incredible journey for me and wouldn't have been possible without the help of many dedicated people.

If it weren't for my incredible Living Rich With Coupons team, I wouldn't have had the time to sit down and write this book. They kept the site rockin' and rollin' with all the latest and hottest deals and tips while I continued to write.

And then there's Toni Robino of Windword Literary Services, my incredible writing coach. You are a guide, a cheerleader, a time manager, and a friend all rolled into one. Thank you for your tireless efforts to get this book completed.

CPSIA information can be obtained at www.ICGtesting.com
Printed in the USA
LVOW10s2117281115

464373LV00004B/14/P

9 781941 729090